science for a changing world

Geologic Assessment of Undiscovered Conventional Oil and Gas Resources—Middle Eocene Claiborne Group, United States Part of the Gulf of Mexico Basin

By Paul C. Hackley

U.S. Geological Survey Open-File Report 2012–1144

U.S. Department of the Interior
U.S. Geological Survey

U.S. Department of the Interior
KEN SALAZAR, Secretary

U.S. Geological Survey
Marcia K. McNutt, Director

U.S. Geological Survey, Reston, Virginia 2012

For product and ordering information:
World Wide Web: *http://www.usgs.gov/pubprod*
Telephone: 1-888-ASK-USGS

For more information on the USGS—the Federal source for science about the Earth,
its natural and living resources, natural hazards, and the environment:
World Wide Web: *http://www.usgs.gov*
Telephone: 1-888-ASK-USGS

Contents

Figures

Table

Geologic Assessment of Undiscovered Conventional Oil and Gas Resources—Middle Eocene Claiborne Group, United States Part of the Gulf of Mexico Basin

By Paul C. Hackley

Abstract

The Middle Eocene Claiborne Group was assessed using established U.S. Geological Survey (USGS) assessment methodology for undiscovered conventional hydrocarbon resources as part of the 2007 USGS assessment of Paleogene-Neogene strata of the United States part of the Gulf of Mexico Basin including onshore and State waters. The assessed area is within the Upper Jurassic-Cretaceous-Tertiary Composite total petroleum system, which was defined as part of the assessment. Source rocks for Claiborne oil accumulations are interpreted to be organic-rich downdip shaley facies of the Wilcox Group and the Sparta Sand of the Claiborne Group; gas accumulations may have originated from multiple sources including the Jurassic Smackover and Haynesville Formations and Bossier Shale, the Cretaceous Eagle Ford and Pearsall(?) Formations, and the Paleogene Wilcox Group and Sparta Sand. Hydrocarbon generation in the basin started prior to deposition of Claiborne sediments and is ongoing at present. Emplacement of hydrocarbons into Claiborne reservoirs has occurred primarily via vertical migration along fault systems; long-range lateral migration also may have occurred in some locations. Primary reservoir sands in the Claiborne Group include, from oldest to youngest, the Queen City Sand, Cook Mountain Formation, Sparta Sand, Yegua Formation, and the laterally equivalent Cockfield Formation. Hydrocarbon traps dominantly are rollover anticlines associated with growth faults; salt structures and stratigraphic traps also are important. Sealing lithologies probably are shaley facies within the Claiborne and in the overlying Jackson Group.

A geologic model, supported by spatial analysis of petroleum geology data including discovered reservoir depths, thicknesses, temperatures, porosities, permeabilities, and pressures, was used to divide the Claiborne Group into seven assessment units (AU) with distinctive structural and depositional settings. The AUs include (1) Lower Claiborne Stable Shelf Gas and Oil (50470120), (2) Lower Claiborne Expanded Fault Zone Gas (50470121), (3) Lower Claiborne Slope and Basin Floor Gas (50470122), (4) Lower Claiborne Cane River (50470123), (5) Upper Claiborne Stable Shelf Gas and Oil (50470124), (6) Upper Claiborne Expanded Fault Zone Gas (50470125), and (7) Upper Claiborne Slope and Basin Floor Gas (50470126). Total estimated mean undiscovered conventional hydrocarbon resources in the seven assessment units combined are 52 million barrels of oil, 19.145 trillion cubic feet of natural gas, and 1.205 billion barrels of natural gas liquids.

A recurring theme that emerged from the evaluation of the seven Claiborne AUs is that the great bulk of undiscovered hydrocarbon resources comprise non-associated gas and condensate contained in deep (mostly >12,000 feet), overpressured, structurally complex outer shelf or slope and basin floor reservoirs. The continuing development of these downdip objectives is expected to be the primary focus of exploration activity for the onshore Middle Eocene Gulf Coast in the coming decades.

Acknowledgments

Discussions with the USGS National Oil and Gas Assessment review committee (T.R. Klett, C.J. Schenk, R.R. Charpentier, and R.M. Pollastro) during the geologic review and assessment meetings guided the analysis of numbers and sizes of undiscovered reservoirs in the Claiborne Group. S.A. Kinney provided GIS support and processing of geospatial information related to the delineation of the assessment units, and for the structure and depth maps of the Claiborne across the basin. J.L. Coleman conceptualized the geologic model, and M. Merrill helped with drafting the geologic model figure. M.S. Hopkins assisted in delineating data subsets from the commercial databases. Critical reviews by S.M. Condon and J.L. Coleman of the USGS and T.E. Ewing of Frontera Exploration Consultants, Inc., greatly improved the quality and clarity of this report. For their leadership and for the sharing of their ideas and geologic experience, the author is indebted to the other members of the Gulf Coast Basin assessment team (L.H. Biewick, J.L. Coleman, S.M. Condon, R.F. Dubiel, D.O. Hayba, A.W. Karlsen, M.A. Keller, M.D. Lewan, P.H. Nelson, O. Pearson, J.K. Pitman, J.L. Ridgley, E.L. Rowan, S.M. Swanson, and P.D. Warwick). N. Kvehnle of Big Joe Operating Company, G. Hepner of McGowan Partners, S. Maley of Badger Oil, and J. King of Josey Oil shared their insights regarding Claiborne and other Gulf Coast hydrocarbon production.

Introduction

The U.S. Geological Survey (USGS) currently is assessing undiscovered oil and gas resources of priority basins within the United States as an update to the comprehensive 1995 national assessment of oil and gas resources (Gautier and others, 1996), which is available from *http://energy.cr.usgs.gov/oilgas/noga/1995.html*. The purpose of this report is to present the results of a geologic assessment of the undiscovered conventional oil and gas resources of the Middle Eocene Claiborne Group in the United States part of the Gulf of Mexico Basin, including onshore and State waters. This report updates the previous report by Hackley (2008), and some of the material contained herein was summarized in the report by Hackley and Ewing (2010).

The Claiborne Group geologic assessment was conducted as part of a geologic assessment of Paleogene-Neogene strata of the onshore United States part of the Gulf of Mexico Basin (Dubiel and others, 2007). The area of the Gulf Basin assessed in this report includes the Western Gulf (Province 5047; Schenk and Viger, 1996a), East Texas (Province 5048; Schenk and Viger, 1996b), and the Louisiana-Mississippi Salt Basins (Province 5049; Schenk and Viger, 1996b) petroleum provinces that were assessed in 1995 (fig. 1). These petroleum provinces were arbitrarily combined into one and numbered 5047 for this assessment. The study area of this report extends northeastward from the border with Mexico on the southwest, through south-central Texas, and eastward into Louisiana, Mississippi, Alabama, and includes a small portion of the Florida panhandle, an area totaling approximately 245,000 square miles. The assessment was conducted using the established methodology of the USGS National Oil and Gas Assessment Project (Klett and others, 2003), in conjunction with literature review and discovery history analysis of proprietary oil and gas production and well databases (IHS Energy Group, 2005a, b), and oil and gas field and reservoir databases (NRG Associates, 2006).

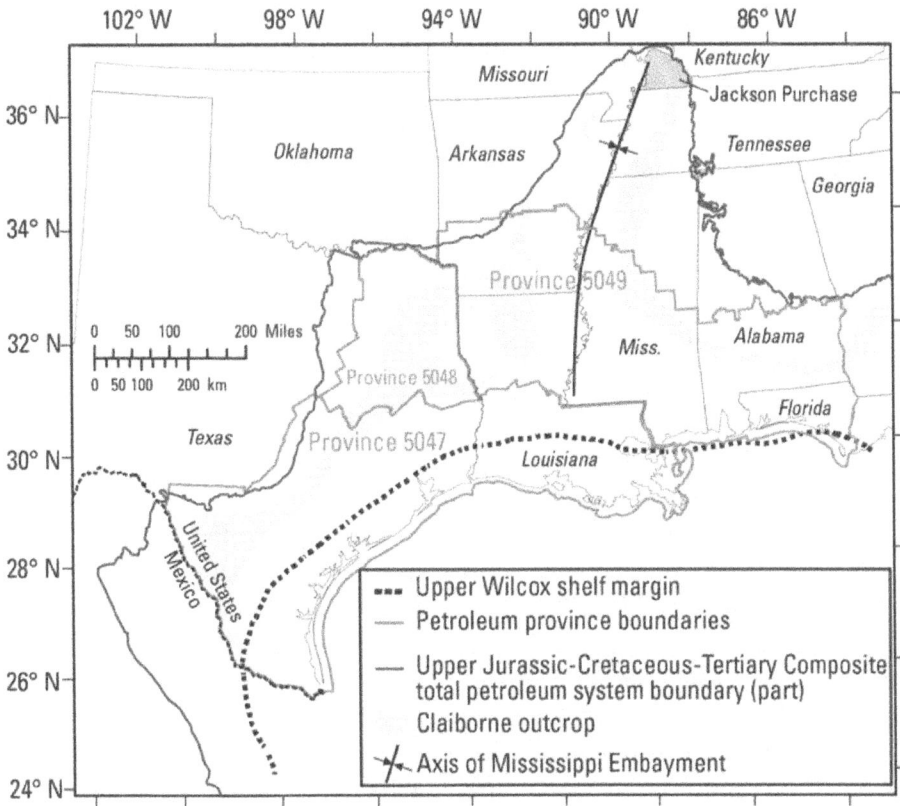

Figure 1. Map of Gulf Coast States showing petroleum province boundaries, outline of Upper Jurassic-Cretaceous-Tertiary Composite total petroleum system (in part), Claiborne Group outcrop (from Schruben and others, 1994), and the upper Wilcox Group shelf margin (from Galloway and others, 2000).

Assessment Unit and Petroleum System Concepts

In this report, assessment units (AU) were used in place of the play concept that was used in the 1995 national assessment. The application of the AU concept is part of the petroleum system approach (described below) to resource assessment (Magoon and Dow, 1994). An AU is "a mappable part of a total petroleum system in which discovered and undiscovered oil and gas accumulations constitute a single relatively homogeneous population such that the methodology of resource assessment is applicable" (Klett, 2004, p. 599). In other words, an AU comprises a three-dimensional volume of rock which contains discovered and undiscovered hydrocarbon resources that are relatively similar in terms of their geological occurrence, exploration strategy, and risk characteristics (Ahlbrandt, 2000). Using AUs in place of the play concept may not necessarily result in quantitative differences in the volumes of undiscovered resources (Klett, 2004), but it supplies a common basis for resource assessment methodology within the USGS (Condon and Dyman, 2006).

The petroleum system approach to resource assessment (Magoon and Dow, 1994) includes an analysis of "genetically related petroleum generated by a pod or by closely related pods of mature source rock" (Condon and Dyman, 2006, p. 2). In this assessment, a composite total petroleum system was defined: the Upper Jurassic-Cretaceous-Tertiary Composite (Warwick and others, 2007). The term "composite" indicates that hydrocarbons reservoired in Gulf Coast Tertiary units were generated from more than one source rock, primarily Jurassic basinal units including the

Smackover and Haynesville Formations and the Bossier Shale, the Cretaceous Eagle Ford and Pearsall(?) Formations, and the Paleogene Wilcox Group and Sparta Sand, although other Gulf of Mexico strata also may have hydrocarbon source potential (fig. 2). The composite total petroleum system includes all of the geologic elements such as source, reservoir, seal, and overburden rocks, which control the processes of generation, migration, and trapping of hydrocarbon resources (Magoon and Dow, 1994; Klett, 2004). A map showing the outline of the Upper Jurassic-Cretaceous-Tertiary Composite total petroleum system of the Gulf of Mexico Basin comprises the total geographic extent of source and reservoir rocks (fig. 3). The outline of the petroleum system is roughly coincident with the outline of the structural limits of the Gulf of Mexico Basin as defined by Salvador (1991a), with some exceptions.

Data Sources and Discovery History Analysis

The Claiborne petroleum geology interpretations presented in this report are based on discovery history analysis of the spatial distribution of wells and known hydrocarbon reservoirs within a geographic information system (GIS). Spatial locations of Claiborne wells from IHS Energy Group (2005a, b) and Claiborne hydrocarbon reservoirs from NRG Associates (2006) were examined using ESRI (Environmental Systems Research Institute, Inc) ArcMap 9.1–9.3. Data from these commercial databases are subject to proprietary license restrictions, and the USGS cannot publish, share, or serve any data from these databases. However, derivative representations in the form of graphs, figures, and summary statistics may be prepared and are presented in this report. Other geologic data used in this assessment include the locations of Claiborne outcrop (Schruben and others, 1994; Warwick and others, 2002), major structural features of the Gulf Basin, faults, and salt (Ewing and Lopez, 1991; Lopez and Orgeron, 1995), geochemical data (Hood and others, 2002), Cenozoic depositional systems and shelf margins (Galloway and others, 2000), regional cross sections, (Dodge and Posey, 1981; Bebout and Gutiérrez, 1982, 1983; Eversull, 1984; Galloway and others, 1994), Claiborne isopach and structure maps (constructed from proprietary data contained in the IHS and NRG Associates databases), oil and gas field executive reference maps (Geomap, 1995a-c), and tectonic maps (Ewing and others, 1990). As an example of the spatial analysis, separation of Claiborne production well and reservoir data into AUs with different geologic characteristics (stable shelf versus expanded fault zone) was completed through an evaluation of discovered reservoir depths, porosity-permeability-pressure-temperature characteristics, and reservoir thicknesses, in comparison with the distribution of reservoirs in the GIS. In addition to analysis of Claiborne petroleum geology within the GIS, the interpretations contained in this report are based on data and interpretations contained in the voluminous published literature on Gulf of Mexico petroleum geology and from conversations and correspondence with industry personnel involved with production from Claiborne reservoirs.

Regional Geologic and Structural Setting

Opening of the Gulf of Mexico Basin began during the Late Triassic due to lithospheric attenuation associated with the breakup of the Pangean supercontinent (Goldthwaite, 1991; Salvador, 1991b). Emplacement of oceanic crust in the now deep, central portions of the Gulf Basin occurred by the Late Jurassic (Buffler, 1991). Earliest basin fill was made up of continental red beds associated with horst and graben structures (Eagle Mills Formation in the subsurface; fig. 2), followed by extensive evaporite deposition of the Callovian (Jurassic) Louann Salt (fig. 2) during a period of restricted basin circulation (Salvador, 1991b). Creation of hydrocarbon

PERIOD	EPOCH	AGE Ma	GROUP OR FORMATION	GAS	OIL	POT. SOURCE ROCK Shale	Coal
QUAT.	HOLO.	—0.01—		△	○		
QUAT.	PLEI.	Calabrian —2.6—	Undifferentiated	△	○		
TERTIARY / NEOGENE	PLIOCENE	Piacenzian Zanclean —5.3—	Undifferentiated	△	○		
TERTIARY / NEOGENE	MIOCENE	Messinian Tortonian Serravallian Langhian Burdigalian Aquitanian —23.0—	Fleming Fm.	△	○		
TERTIARY / PALEOGENE	OLIGOCENE	Chattian —28.4—	Catahoula Fm. Anahuac Fm. Frio Fm.	△	○		
TERTIARY / PALEOGENE	OLIGOCENE	Rupelian —33.9—	Vicksburg Grp.	△	○	■	☆
TERTIARY / PALEOGENE	EOCENE	Priabonian —37.2—	Jackson Grp.	△	○	■	☆
TERTIARY / PALEOGENE	EOCENE	Bartonian Lutetian —48.6—	Claiborne Grp.	△	○	■	☆
TERTIARY / PALEOGENE	EOCENE	Ypresian —55.8—	Wilcox Grp.	△	○	■	☆ Important source rock
TERTIARY / PALEOGENE	PAL	Thanetian Selandian Danian —65.5—	Midway Grp.			■	
CRETACEOUS / UPPER		Maastrichtian —70.6—	Navarro Grp. (Olmos Fm.-Escondido Fm.)	△	○		☆
CRETACEOUS / UPPER		Campanian —83.5—	Taylor Grp. (Anacacho Ls./ San Miguel Fm./ Ozan Fm./Annona Ch.)	△	○	■	
CRETACEOUS / UPPER		Santonian Coniacian —89.3—	Austin Grp./Tokio Fm./ Eutaw Fm.	△	○	■	
CRETACEOUS / UPPER		Turonian Cenomanian —99.6—	Eagle Ford Fm. Woodbine Fm./Tuscaloosa Grp.	△	○	■ Important source rock	
CRETACEOUS / LOWER		Albian	Washita Grp. (Buda Ls.)	△			
CRETACEOUS / LOWER		Albian	Fredricksburg Grp. (Edwards Ls./Paluxy Fm.)	△	○		
CRETACEOUS / LOWER		Albian —112—	Glen Rose Fm. (Rodessa Fm.)	△	○	■	
CRETACEOUS / LOWER			Pearsall Fm.	△	○	?	
CRETACEOUS / LOWER		Aptian	Sligo Fm. (Pettet Fm.)	△	○		
CRETACEOUS / LOWER		Barremian Hauterivian —125— —136—	Hosston Fm. (Travis Peak Fm.)	△	○	■	☆
CRETACEOUS / LOWER		Valanginian Berriasian —145.5—	Cotton Valley Fm.	△	○	■	
JURASSIC / UPPER		Tithonian —151—	Cotton Valley Fm. Bossier Fm.	△	○	■	Important
JURASSIC / UPPER		Kimmeridgian —156—	Haynesville Fm./ Gilmer Ls.	△	○	■	
JURASSIC / UPPER		Oxfordian —161—	Smackover Fm. Norphlet Fm.	△	○	■	source rock
JURASSIC / MID.		Callovian Bathonian	Louann Salt Werner Fm.		○		
JURASSIC / L.		Hettangian —197—					
TRIA. / UP.		Rhaetian Norian Carnian —201.6—	Eagle Mills Fm.			■	

Figure 2. Generalized stratigraphic section of the northern Gulf of Mexico Coastal Plain showing potential hydrocarbon source rock intervals (from Hackley and Ewing (2010); modified after Warwick and others (2007), Salvador and Quezada Muñeton (1991), Nehring (1991), Palmer and Geissman (1999), and Humble Geochemical Services and others (2002)). L. = Lower, Mid. = Middle, Up. = Upper, Tria. = Triassic, Pal. = Paleocene, Plei. = Pleistocene, Holo. = Holocene, Quat. = Quaternary, vertical lines = unconformity, wavy line = disconformity, jagged line = interfingering, dashed line = uncertain.

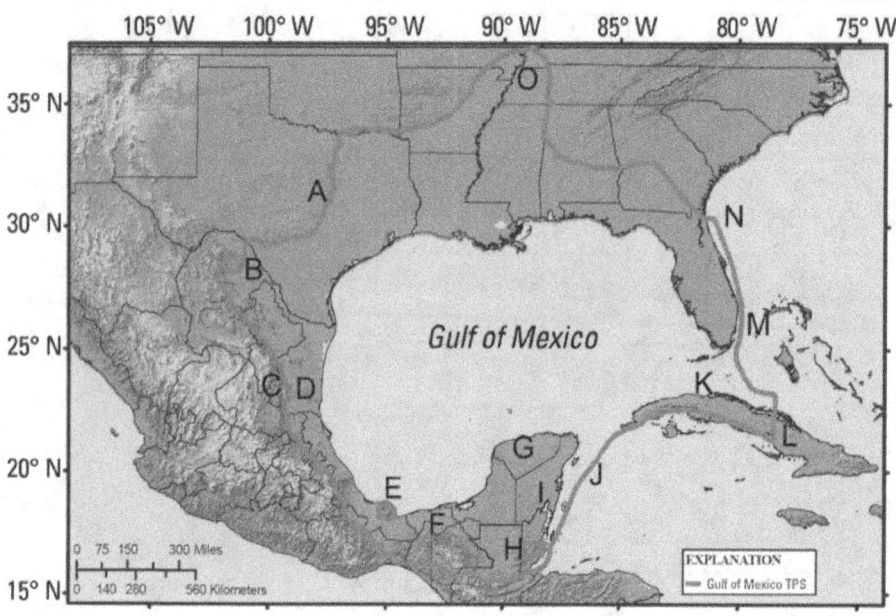

Figure 3. Upper Jurassic-Cretaceous-Tertiary Composite total petroleum system (TPS) for the Gulf of Mexico Basin. The letters (A-O) refer to the following notes on how the TPS boundary was drawn. A, coincides with the outcrop contact between Upper and Lower Cretaceous rocks (Schruben and others, 1994); this line may be somewhat arbitrary, as the area may include some Interior Platform Paleozoic-derived oil that has migrated into Cretaceous reservoirs and is not part of the Gulf of Mexico TPS. B, includes both Maverick and Sabinas Basins, which have Gulf of Mexico Basin source and reservoir rocks (Eguiluz de Antuñano, 2001; Scott, 2003). C, excludes Sierra Madre Oriental, which has stratigraphic equivalents to Gulf of Mexico Basin source and reservoir rocks but probably has experienced too much structural deformation and erosion to retain any significant hydrocarbon volumes (Ewing, 1991). D, includes the Magiscatzin Basin, which has production from units of the main Tampico-Misantla Basin and contains similar strata and structural styles as found in the Gulf of Mexico Basin (Nehring, 1991; USGS World Energy Assessment Team, 2000). E, excludes Tuxla Uplift, an Upper Cenozoic volcanic area (Ewing, 1991). F, includes the Pimienta-Tamabra TPS (USGS World Energy Assessment Team, 2000). G, includes north Yucatan because hydrocarbons are present in Chicxulub Crater cores (Rosenfeld, 2003). H, excludes the Maya Mountains, a metamorphic orogenic complex (Ewing, 1991; Ewing and Lopez, 1991). I, includes the south Yucatan because of the occurrence of isolated oil and gas production and shows (Rosenfeld, 2003). J, line drawn along major sea-floor crustal structural boundary between oceanic crust in the Yucatan Basin and back-arc Cuban basins and oceanic crust in the Greater Antilles Deformed Belt (Ewing, 1991; Rodriguez and others, 1995; James, 2004; Schenk and others, 2005). K, includes north Cuba, where there are the same source rocks as in South Florida and the deep-water Gulf of Mexico (Schenk and others, 2000, 2005; French and Schenk, 2004). L, follows an arbitrary limit to the TPS in the Gulf of Mexico Basin. M, follows an arbitrary line drawn to separate the Bahamas from the Florida Platform (Ewing, 1991). N, follows the Smackover-Austin-Eagle Ford TPS boundary of Condon and Dyman (2006); however, the potential occurrence of source rocks and hydrocarbons in this area is highly speculative. O, the Mississippi Embayment includes Tertiary and Cretaceous coal beds as potential sources of biogenic gas, although there is no known hydrocarbon production from this area. For additional information on construction of the TPS outline see French and Schenk (2005).

migration pathways and trapping structures by diapiric and related evacuation movements of the Louann Salt due to sediment loading is one of the controlling aspects of Gulf Coast petroleum geology (Halbouty, 1979; Wescott and Hood, 1994). Cenozoic basin fill comprises almost exclusively terrigenous clastics originating from North America, except for areas of carbonate and evaporate deposition, which occurred on the Florida and Yucatan Platforms, and in parts of Mississippi, Alabama, and Georgia (Galloway and others, 1991). Strata are well to poorly lithified, depending on age, depth of burial, fluid flow, and hydrochemistry and dip gently to moderately (on domal margins) basinward (except where they dip northward off structural culminations). Gulf strata in the United States generally are undeformed except for the effects of syndepositional growth faulting and salt tectonics.

Clastic depositional centers migrated from southwest to northeast across the northern part of the basin during the Cenozoic (Thompson and others, 1990; Mello and Karner, 1996; Galloway and others, 2000), controlled by tectonism and the climatic conditions prevailing on the continent (Galloway, 2005). In the particular focus of this report, Middle Eocene clastic deposition of the Claiborne Group includes progradational sand-rich wedges that grade basinward into marine mudrocks. Progradational strata of the Claiborne, including the Queen City Sand, Sparta Sand, and the Yegua and Cockfield Formations, are separated by marine shales (Reklaw, Weches, Cook Mountain Formations) deposited during regional transgression and flooding of the continental margin (fig. 4) (Davies and Ethridge, 1971; Ramos and Galloway, 1990; Galloway and others, 2000). In terms of total sediment volume input to the basin and input rate, the Claiborne Group is a comparatively minor unit compared to other intervals of the Gulf of Mexico Cenozoic stratigraphy (Galloway and others, 2000; Galloway, 2002). In particular, Frio strata overlying the Claiborne dominate the Paleogene Gulf in volume and rate of sediment input (Galloway, 2002, 2005), as well as in historical oil and gas production (Nehring, 1991).

Structural Setting

The distribution of the Claiborne Group lies across all of the major structural features of the northern part of the Gulf of Mexico Basin (fig. 5). Proceeding northeastward from the United States-Mexico border in the downdip basinward subsurface, these include the Rio Grande Embayment, the San Marcos Arch, the Houston Embayment, and the South Louisiana Salt Basin. Updip, in the northern part of the basin, Claiborne outcrop lies athwart the East Texas Basin and the Sabine Uplift, from which most of the Claiborne is eroded. The outcrop belt follows the Mississippi Embayment northward through Louisiana into Arkansas and southern Missouri before wrapping south through the Jackson Purchase area of western Kentucky and into western Tennessee (fig. 1). The outcrop parallels Cretaceous strata around the southern end of the Appalachians southward through Mississippi and eastward into Alabama, then wrapping northeastward through southern Georgia out of the Gulf Basin and into the Atlantic Coastal Plain. The Claiborne is present in the subsurface south of the outcrop belt across the entirety of the onshore part of the Gulf Basin, except on the Wiggins Uplift in southern Mississippi (fig. 5) and potentially on the crests of some salt domes. In the subsurface of the northern and eastern parts of the basin, the distribution of the Claiborne Group is influenced by the structures of the North Louisiana Salt Basin, the Monroe Uplift and La Salle Arch, and the Mississippi Salt Basin. The downdip limit of the Claiborne has not been well delineated by drilling; few complete penetrations of the Claiborne Group occur basinward of the upper Wilcox shelf margin (fig. 1) (T.E. Ewing, Frontera Exploration Consultants, Inc., written commun., 2008).

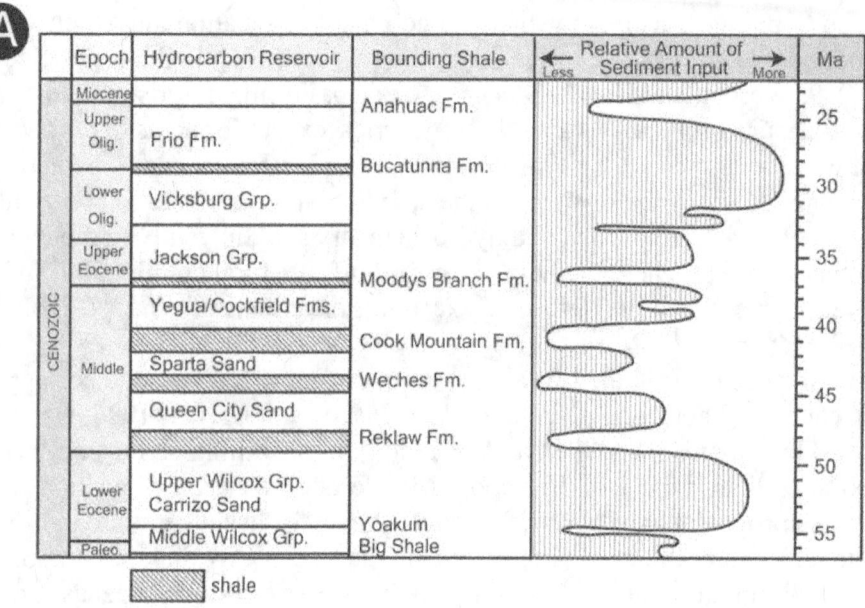

A

Epoch	Hydrocarbon Reservoir	Bounding Shale	Relative Amount of Sediment Input (Less → More)	Ma
Miocene		Anahuac Fm.		
Upper Olig.	Frio Fm.			25
		Bucatunna Fm.		30
Lower Olig.	Vicksburg Grp.			
Upper Eocene	Jackson Grp.	Moodys Branch Fm.		35
Middle	Yegua/Cockfield Fms.	Cook Mountain Fm.		40
	Sparta Sand	Weches Fm.		45
	Queen City Sand	Reklaw Fm.		
Lower Eocene	Upper Wilcox Grp. Carrizo Sand			50
	Middle Wilcox Grp.	Yoakum		55
Paleo.		Big Shale		

(CENOZOIC)

▨ shale

B

EPOCH	GROUP		TEXAS — Southern	TEXAS — Southeastern and Northeastern	LOUISIANA
Eocene	Claiborne Group	Upper	Yegua Fm. ☼ ● S? (Pettus Sand) (O'Hern Sand) (Rosenburg Sand) (Bruni Sand)	Yegua Fm. ☼ ● S?	Cockfield Fm. ☼ ● S?
		Middle	Laredo Fm. — Cook Mt. Fm. ☼ ● S? (Crockett Fm.) / Sparta Sand ☼ ● S?	Cook Mt. Fm. ☼ ● S? (Crockett Fm.) / Sparta Sand ☼ ● S?	Cook Mt. Fm. ☼ ● S? / Sparta Sand ☼ ● S?
		Lower	El Pico Clay — Weches Fm. / Queen City Sand ☼ ● S? / Bigford Fm. — Reklaw Fm. ☼ ● S? (First Reklaw-Atkinson Sand) (Second Reklaw Sand)	Weches Fm. / Queen City Sand ☼ ● S? (Mt. Selman Fm.) / Reklaw Fm. ☼ ● S?	Cane River Fm.
			Carrizo Sand ☼ ● S?		
Paleocene			☼ Gas reservoir / ● Oil reservoir / S? Postulated source rock	Wilcox Group undifferentiated ☼ ● S?	

Figure 4. Stratigraphy of the Claiborne Group. A, stratigraphic column showing main hydrocarbon reservoir rocks, bounding shale packages, and relative volumes of sediment input to the northern Gulf of Mexico during the Paleogene (from Galloway and others, 2000). Fm. = Formation, Fms. = Formations, Grp. = Group, Paleo.=Paleocene, Olig. = Oligocene. B, regional stratigraphic nomenclature for the Claiborne Group in south Texas, southeastern-northeastern Texas, and in Louisiana (from Guevara and García, 1972; Sams, 1990; Wescott and Hood, 1994; Schenk and Viger, 1996a; Hosman, 1996; and Warwick and others, 2002). Names in parentheses are or were used locally. The Yegua/Cockfield Formations and Sparta and Queen City Sands are sand-rich conventional oil and gas reservoirs at the historical depths of exploration and production in the northern Gulf of Mexico Basin. However, downdip, organic-rich shaley facies of Wilcox Group and the Reklaw Formation, Queen City Sand, Sparta Sand, Cook Mountain Formation, Yegua Formation, and Cockfield Formations of the Claiborne Group all have been postulated potential source rocks at depth and therefore are indicated with "S?".

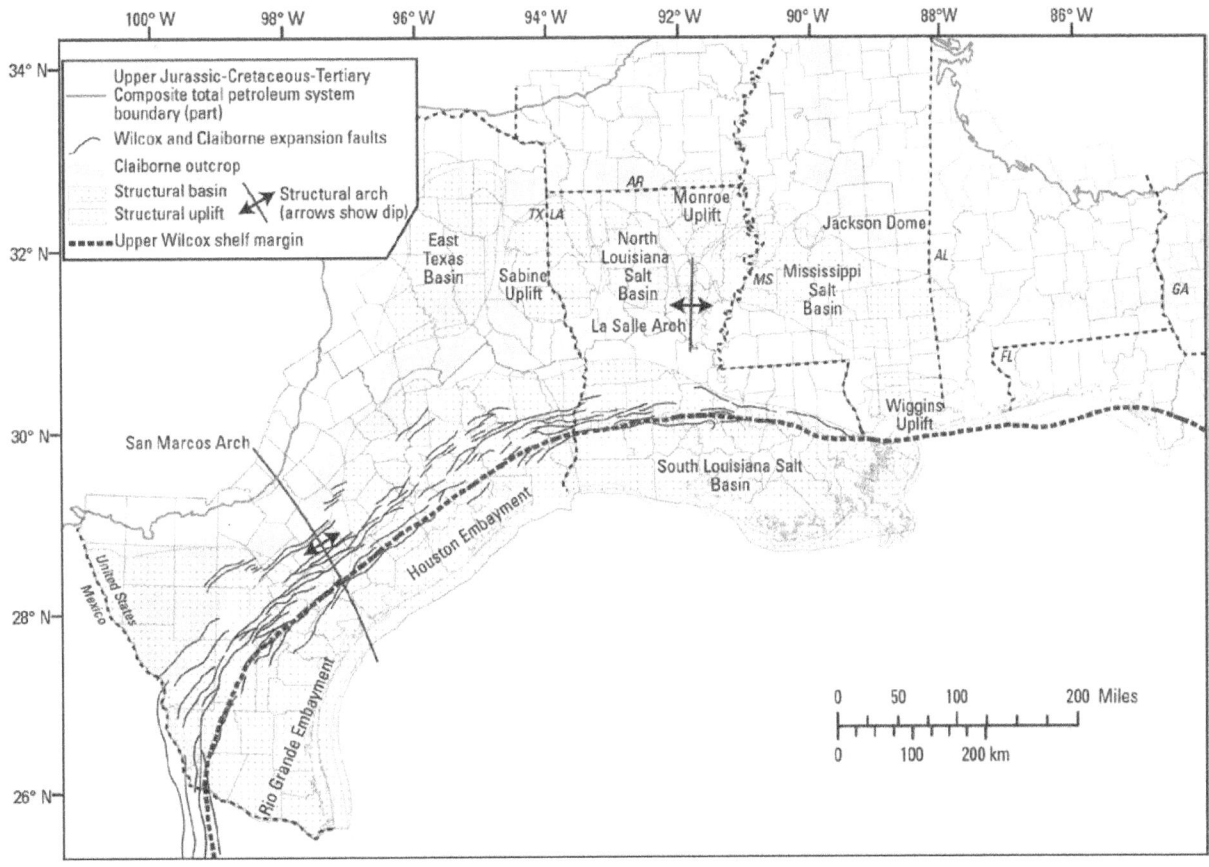

Figure 5. Map of study area (onshore U.S. Gulf Coast and State waters) showing Claiborne Group outcrop, Wilcox and Claiborne expansion faults, and outline of major structural features. Claiborne Group outcrop is from Schruben and others (1994); major structural features and faults are from Ewing and Lopez (1991); Wilcox shelf edge is from Galloway and others (2000).

The majority of Claiborne oil and gas production is from fields in the three major downdip structural provinces, the Rio Grande Embayment, the Houston Embayment, and the South Louisiana Salt Basin (fig. 6). One exception to this trend is hydrocarbon production from the Sparta Sand in central Louisiana and southern Mississippi on the downdip margin of the La Salle arch and the North Louisiana Salt Basin. Although some downdip Claiborne gas production is from over 14,000 feet (ft) in depth in Jefferson County, Tex., the main productive trend is from depths of 6,000 to 9,000 ft across Texas and Louisiana (fig. 7). Claiborne production across the onshore Gulf Coast region primarily is gas, but oil accumulations are present as well, particularly in the updip part of the trend.

Movement of salt diapirs and other salt features primarily impacts the structure of the Claiborne Group in the subsurface of the Houston Embayment and South Louisiana Salt Basin. Claiborne hydrocarbon resources associated with salt commonly are found in anticlinal folds and domes over deeper salt (Katy, Conroe, Bammel, Raccoon Bend, Tomball fields, Texas) and in stratigraphic pinchouts against and over salt diapirs (Esperson Dome, Hockley fields, Texas) (fig. 6). The Houston Embayment contains approximately 60 known shallow salt diapirs and a few known or inferred salt pillows (Ewing, 1991). Many of the shallower salt diapirs are rootless or

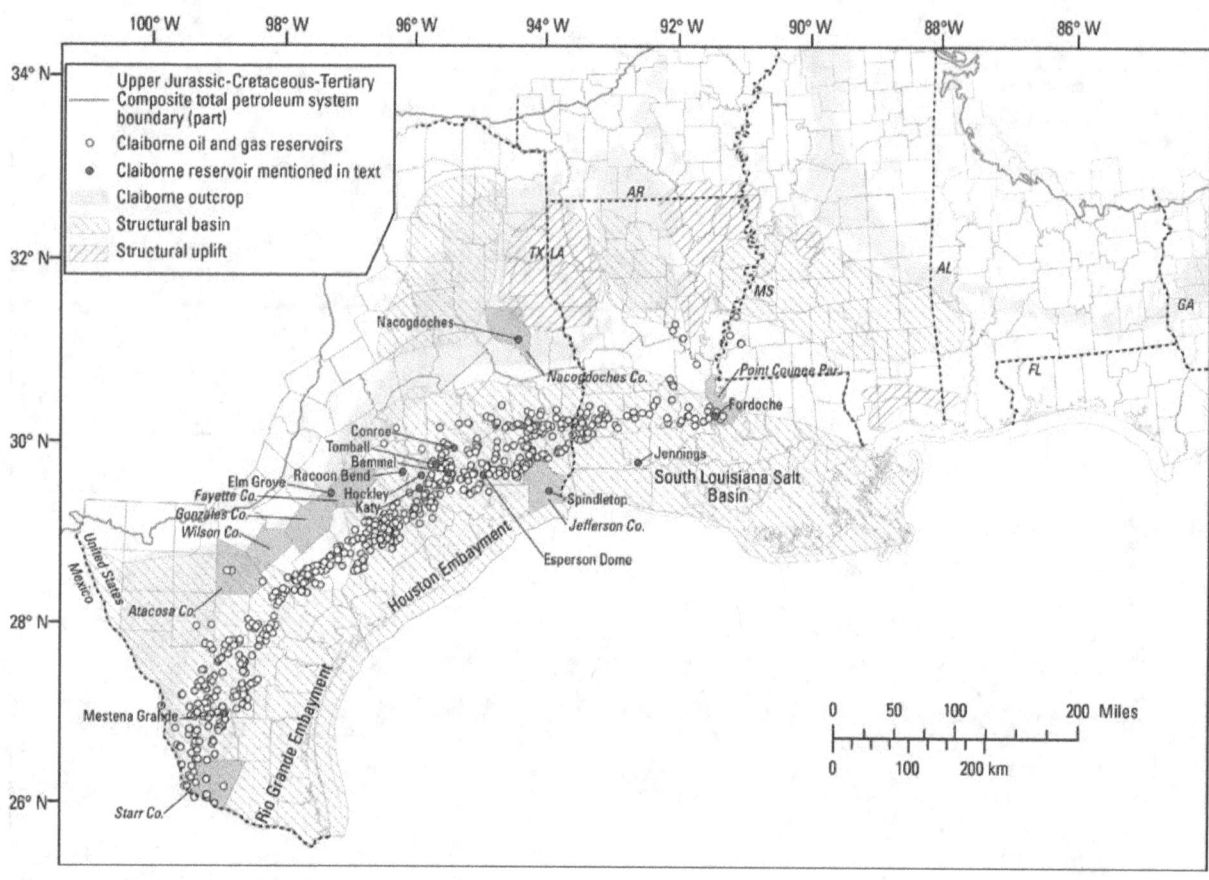

Figure 6. Map of study area showing approximate locations of Claiborne Group oil and gas reservoirs (white circles). Reservoir locations are from NRG Associates (2006). Claiborne Group outcrop is from Schruben and others (1994); major structural features are from Ewing and Lopez (1991). Claiborne Group and other reservoirs discussed in the text are shown as blue circles. Elm Grove, Spindletop, and Jennings fields are discussed herein but were not assessed with Claiborne Group reservoirs, as these fields produce primarily from other intervals. Co.=County.

rooted into salt welds (T.E. Ewing, Frontera Exploration Consultants, Inc., written commun., 2008). Large areas of welds in the Weches horizon are interpreted to indicate a post-Wilcox canopy which deflated under Yegua progradation in southeast Texas (T.E. Ewing, Frontera Exploration Consultants, Inc., written commun., 2008). The South Louisiana Salt Basin contains mostly small, cylindrical, shallow salt diapirs, but more extensive salt ridges and massifs are present, particularly in the southern areas of thick Pliocene-Pleistocene sediment deposition (Ewing, 1991). Salt tectonics have strongly influenced upper Claiborne hydrocarbon systems in southeast Texas and western Louisiana, where salt movement may have disrupted trap formation and shaped sand distribution (Ewing, 2008). The salt basins are separated from the Rio Grande Embayment by the San Marcos Arch, which is defined by a southeastward bowing of the outcrop pattern through strata as young as Eocene (Ewing, 1991).

The Rio Grande Embayment contains a few salt domes, but overall, salt is a minor component of the Cenozoic structural style of the province (Ewing, 1991). Ewing (2008) suggested that deep-seated salt movements may have played some role in Claiborne hydrocarbon systems in

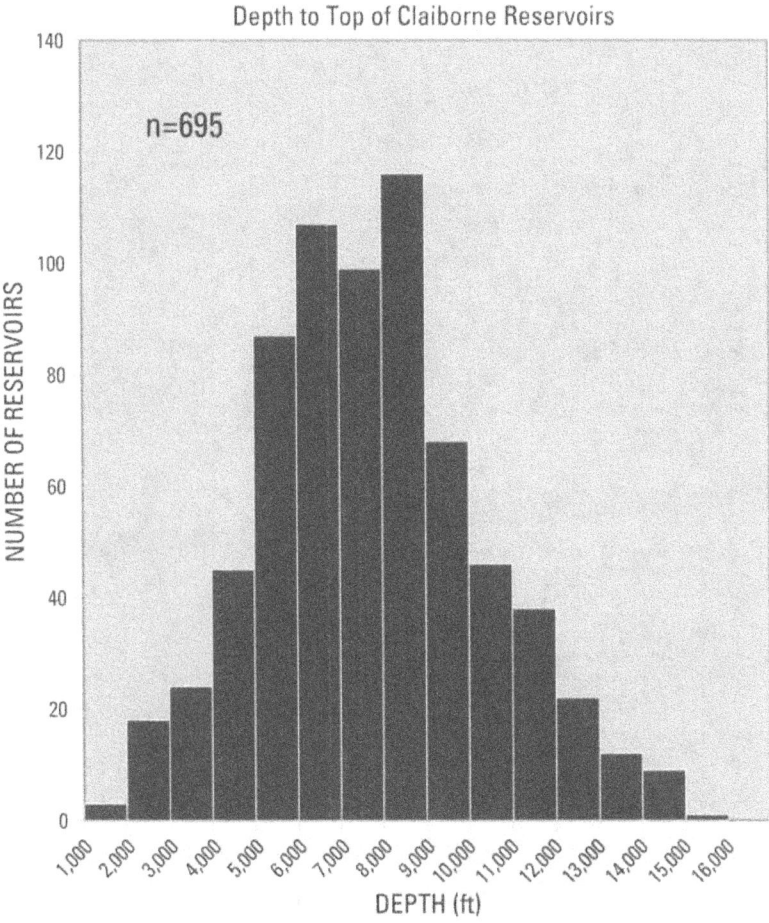

Figure 7. Histogram of depth to top of Claiborne Group reservoirs, Texas and Louisiana. Data are from NRG Associates (2006).

the Rio Grande Embayment but did not indicate specific instances. In the western and southwestern part of the embayment, Laramide compression has developed a series of low-amplitude northwest-trending folds (Ewing, 1991). These folds primarily modify the structure of Mesozoic strata but occur as far to the east as western Starr County in the Claiborne outcrop belt (Ewing, 2008).

The Claiborne Group ranges greatly in overall thickness, varying from less than 700 ft in southeastern Louisiana (Bebout and Gutiérrez, 1983) to over 5,500 ft in south Texas (Dodge and Posey, 1981). The overall sedimentation style was dominated by offlapping progradational wedges where stratigraphic units dip toward the basin and thicken basinward, with maximum thickening basinward of the major depocenters of underlying units (Galloway and others, 1991). An isopach map generated as part of this assessment from stratigraphic tops in the IHS database (IHS Energy Group, 2005b) shows that the thickest Claiborne section is in south Texas (fig. 8). However, data quality in south Texas may be negatively impacted by a paucity of downdip penetrations for the tops of units below the Claiborne. In general, as with other Cenozoic stratigraphic packages, the Claiborne thickens downdip into the Gulf of Mexico Basin over a relatively narrow margin on contemporary growth faults, eventually thinning basinward where sediment supply became scarce. For example, the regional cross sections constructed by Dodge and Posey (1981) show the Claiborne to be approximately 2,500 ft thick in northern Tyler County, in the Houston Embayment

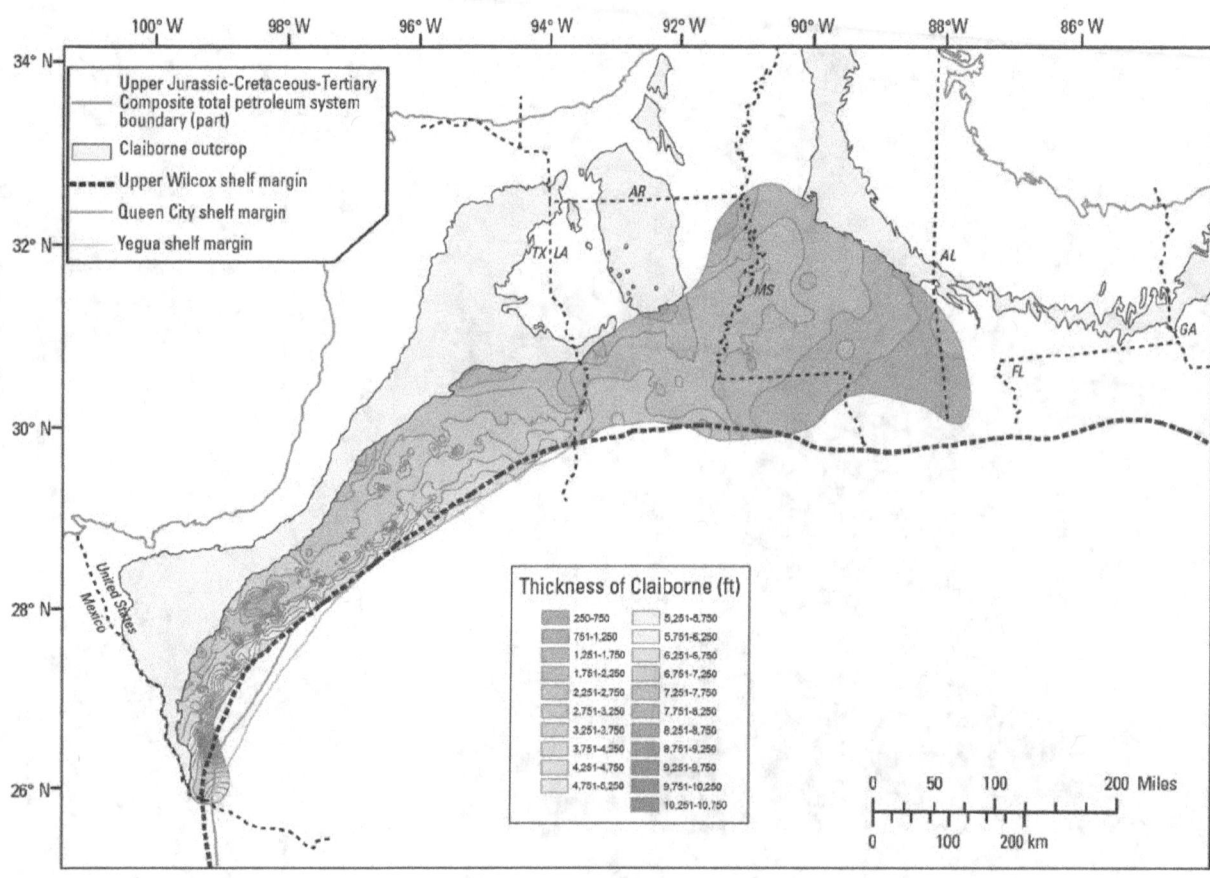

Figure 8. Claiborne Group isopach map constructed from the IHS Energy Group (2005b) database using data current through 2004 and from the Paleo-Data, Inc. (1989) Tenroc Regional Geologic database. Tops data from IHS Energy Group (2005b) were combined with paleontologic data from Paleo-Data, Inc. (1989) in ArcMap 9.1 (Environmental Systems Research Institute, Inc), and a kriging process was used to create a surface grid for formation tops. Isopach thicknesses were determined by subtraction of surface grids or by the subtraction of individual data points where sufficient tops data were present in the databases. Insufficient tops data are available in the IHS and Tenroc databases east of the Mississippi-Alabama State boundary to extend the Claiborne Group isopach farther eastward confidently.

of northeast Texas, thickening southward to approximately 3,750 ft in southern Jasper County (their cross section 1-1'; fig. 9). In the Rio Grande Embayment, the Claiborne thickens southeastward by over 1,300 ft across Webb County (their cross section 21; fig. 10), and by almost 3,000 ft from McMullen into Live Oak County (their cross section 18; fig. 11). Eastward into Louisiana, the Claiborne is approximately 1,875 ft thick in southern Avoyelles Parish on cross section I-I' of Eversull (1984) before thickening basinward on growth faults to approximately 2,775 ft thick in the deepest complete Claiborne penetration, as depicted on cross-section H-H' of Bebout and Gutiérrez (1982) (southward continuation of cross section I-I'). Cross-section R-R', farthest east in Louisiana (Bebout and Gutiérrez, 1983), shows the Claiborne to be approximately 100 ft thick in St. Tammany Parish, rapidly thickening basinward to approximately 700 ft in St. Bernard Parish (fig. 12). The cross sections constructed by Dodge and Posey (1981), Bebout and Gutiérrez (1982, 1983), and Eversull (1984) were based on 1970s-era and earlier drilling; development of the downdip expanded Yegua section beginning in the 1980s indicates that the

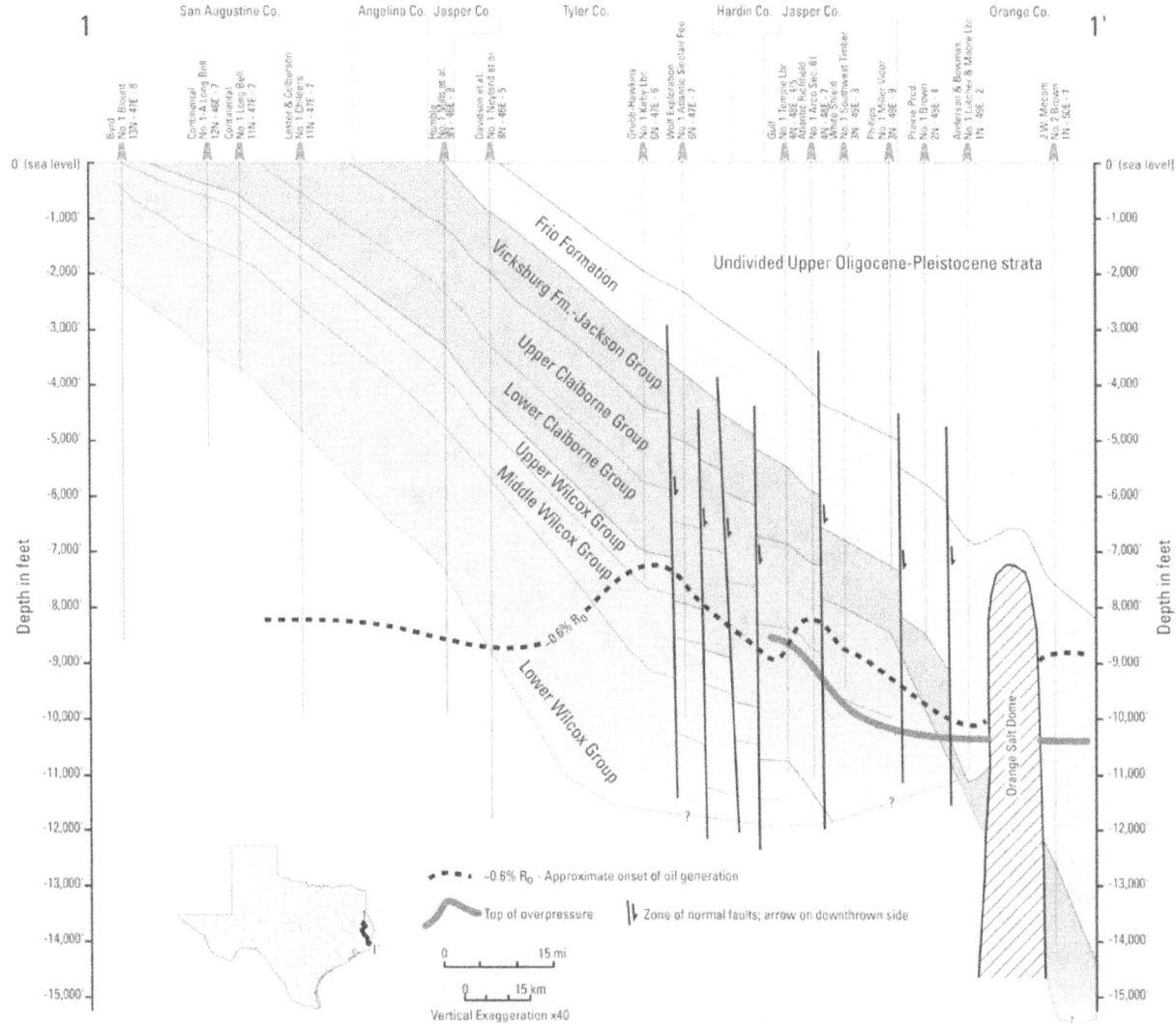

Figure 9. Dodge and Posey (1981) cross section 1-1' in the Houston Embayment. On this section, new drilling (postdating the data used by Dodge and Posey, 1981) documents a thicker downdip Yegua (upper Claiborne) section than shown (T.E. Ewing, Frontera Exploration Consultants, Inc., written commun., 2008). The approximate onset of oil generation at 0.6 percent vitrinite reflectance (R_o) corresponds to the present-day down-hole temperature of 200 °F (93 °C) using the general relationship of R_o to temperature established by Barker and Pawlewicz (1986) from worldwide basins. Faults are generalized and represent zones constituted by multiple individual faults. The line representing the onset of overpressure presumably extends across the entire section through the Wilcox Group; the data for the representation of overpressure on this cross section are from the original publication and are based on mud weights. The annotation for the wells includes the operator name in the first line, the well name and number in the second line, and the township, range, and section in the third line. Fm. = Formation, Co. = County, Lbr. = Lumber.

13

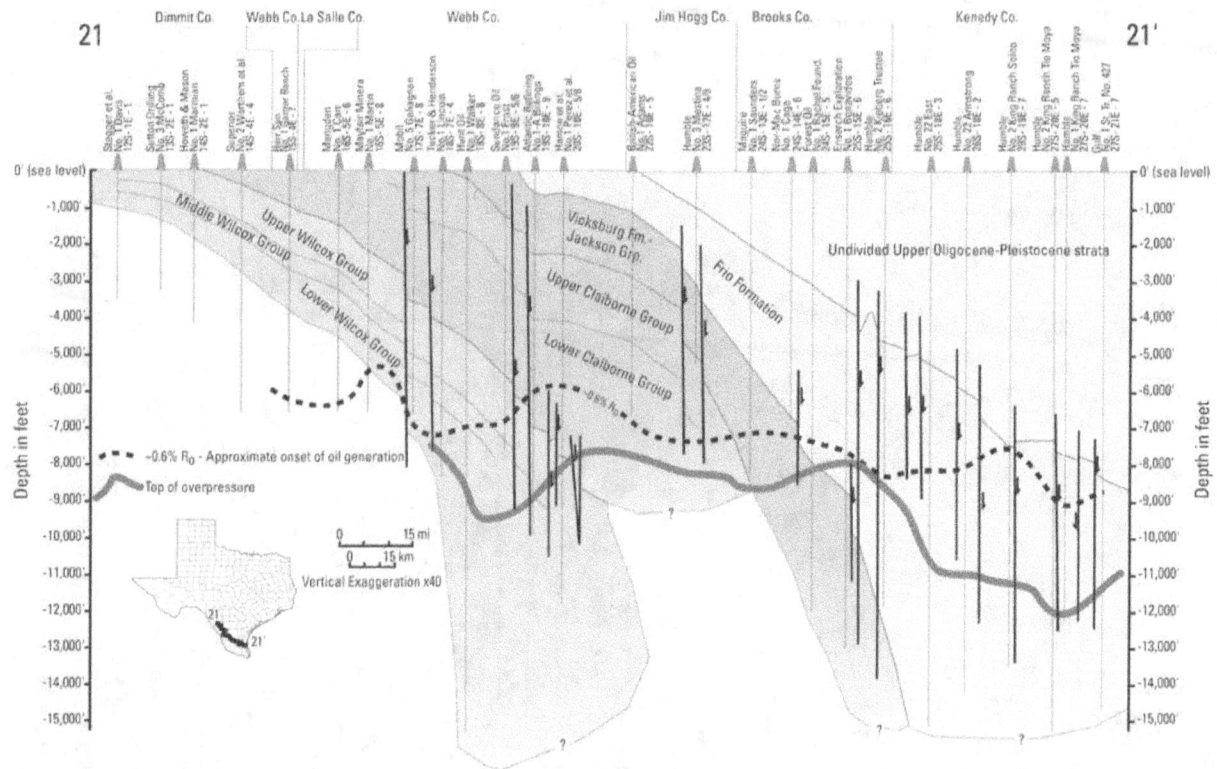

Figure 10. Dodge and Posey (1981) cross section 21-21' in the Rio Grande Embayment. The approximate onset of oil generation at 0.6 percent vitrinite reflectance (R_o) corresponds to the present-day down-hole temperature of 200 °F (93 °C) using the general relationship of R_o to temperature established by Barker and Pawlewicz (1986) from worldwide basins. Faults are generalized and represent zones constituted by multiple individual faults. The data for the representation of overpressure are from the original publication. The annotation for the wells includes the operator name in the first line, the well name and number in the second line, and the township, range, and section in the third line. Drilling still has not determined the downdip extent of the Claiborne section (T.E. Ewing, Frontera Exploration Consultants, Inc., written commun., 2008), although seismic reflectors have been interpreted at the top of the Claiborne in the deepwater Gulf (Fiduk and others, 1999). Fm. = Formation, Grp. = Group, Co. = County.

Claiborne Group is somewhat thicker downdip than revealed in the published regional cross sections (T.E. Ewing, Frontera Exploration Consultants, Inc., written commun., 2008).

A structure map of the top of the Claiborne Group constructed from IHS tops data (IHS Energy Group, 2005b) indicates that depth to the top of the Claiborne rapidly increases basinward of the underlying upper Wilcox shelf margin, which is at 9,000 to 10,000 ft from central Texas eastward into Louisiana (fig. 13). In south Texas, along the Rio Grande Embayment axis (Galloway and others, 2000), the depth to the top of the Yegua (top formation of the Claiborne Group) is at approximately 3,000–6,000 ft at the upper Wilcox shelf margin, where the depth to the top of the Claiborne also rapidly increases basinward. The large difference in the depth to top of the Yegua at the upper Wilcox shelf break indicates that comparatively more post-Yegua sediment has been deposited in Louisiana along the Mississippi Embayment axis, as the nexus of major depocenters gradually migrated northeastward during the Neogene (Galloway and others, 2000;

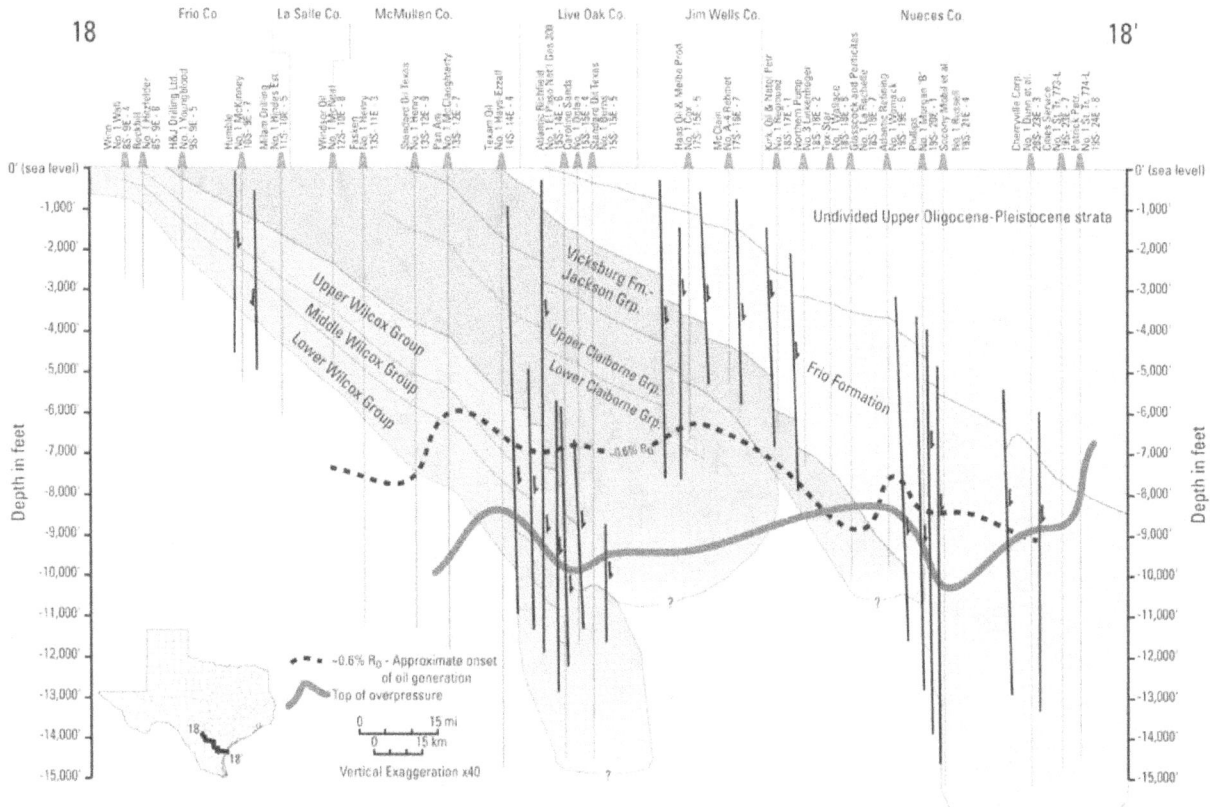

Figure 11. Dodge and Posey (1981) cross section 18-18' in the Rio Grande Embayment. The approximate onset of oil generation at 0.6 percent vitrinite reflectance (R_o) corresponds to the present-day down-hole temperature of 200 °F (93 °C) using the general relationship of R_o to temperature established by Barker and Pawlewicz (1986) from worldwide basins. Faults are generalized and represent zones constituted by multiple individual faults. The data for the representation of overpressure are from the original publication. The annotation for the wells includes the operator name in the first line, the well name and number in the second, and the township, range, and section in the third. Fm. = Formation, Grp. = Group, Co. = County.

Galloway, 2005). In several places within the Houston Embayment and the South Louisiana Salt Basin, the top of the Claiborne shallows substantially over salt domes (fig. 13).

Stratigraphy

The Claiborne Group was deposited over the period of approximately 49 to 37 million years ago (Ma) in the Middle Eocene (Lutetian-Bartonian Stages) (Galloway and others, 2000; Witrock and others, 2003). In much of Texas, the Claiborne is stratigraphically divided into lower, middle, and upper packages of primarily progradational sandstones that are separated from each other by packages of primarily transgressive shales and mudstones (fig. 4).

At the base of the Claiborne, the transgressive Reklaw Formation is characterized by thin interbedded sandstones and shales overlying the massive sands of the Carrizo Sand (fig. 4). Early workers placed the Carrizo Sand in the Wilcox Group (Trowbridge, 1923); however, the Carrizo Sand more recently has been considered the basal unit in the Claiborne Group (Eargle, 1968). The Carrizo Sand was assessed separately from the Claiborne Group in this work and is included with

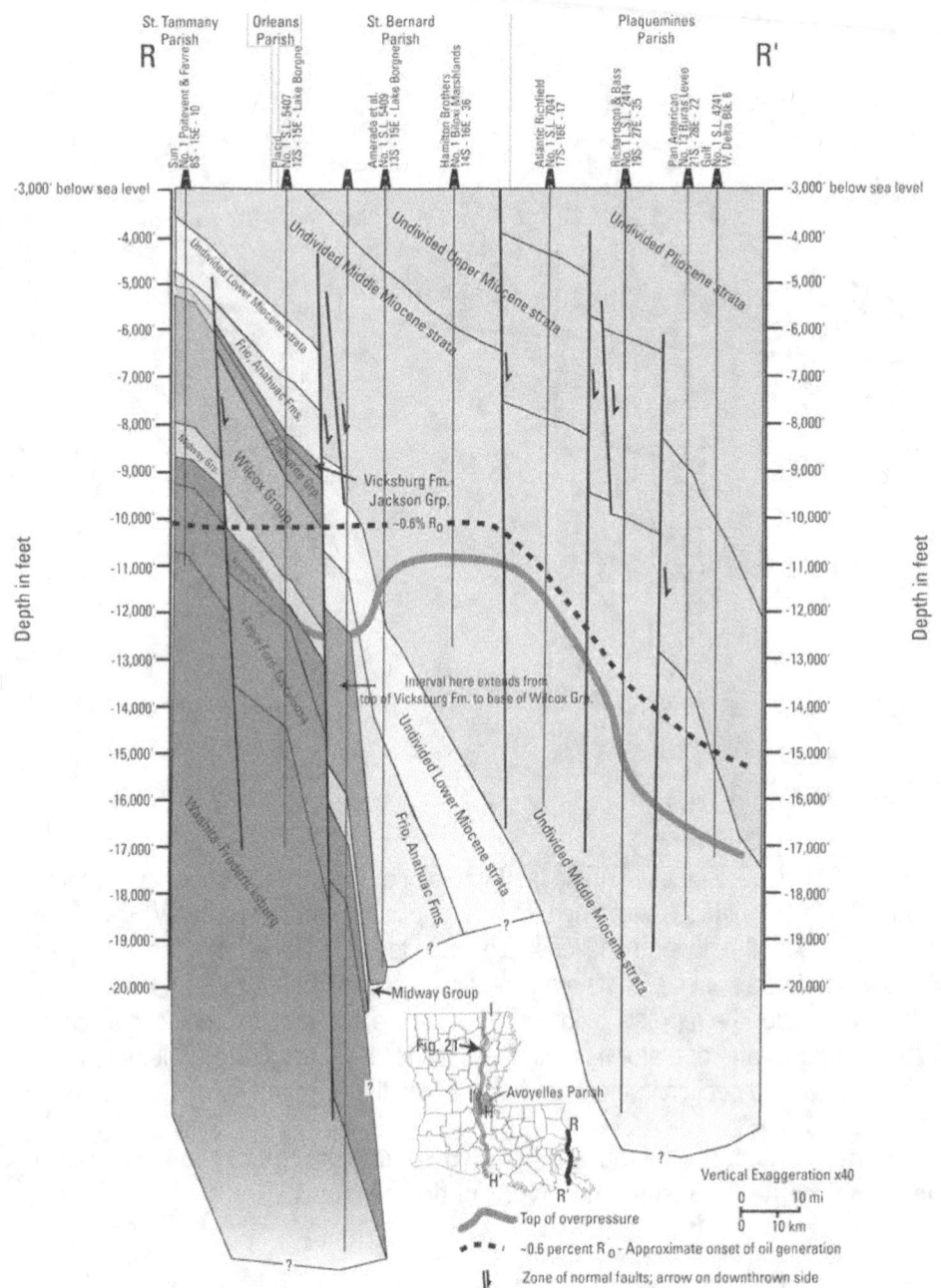

Figure 12. Bebout and Gutiérrez (1983) cross section R-R' in southeastern Louisiana illustrating thinning of the Claiborne, thickness of the Neogene, and the abrupt steepening of the Cenozoic section over the Cretaceous shelf margin in the eastern part of the basin. The approximate onset of oil generation at 0.6 percent vitrinite reflectance (R_o) corresponds to the present-day down-hole temperature of 200 °F (93 °C) using the general relationship of R_o to temperature established by Barker and Pawlewicz (1986) from worldwide basins. The data for the representation of overpressure are from the original publication. The annotation for the wells includes the operator name in the first line, the well name and number in the second, and the township, range, and section in the third. Fm. = Formation, Fms. = Formations, Grp. = Group. Inset shows the line of section for figure 21 of this publication.

16

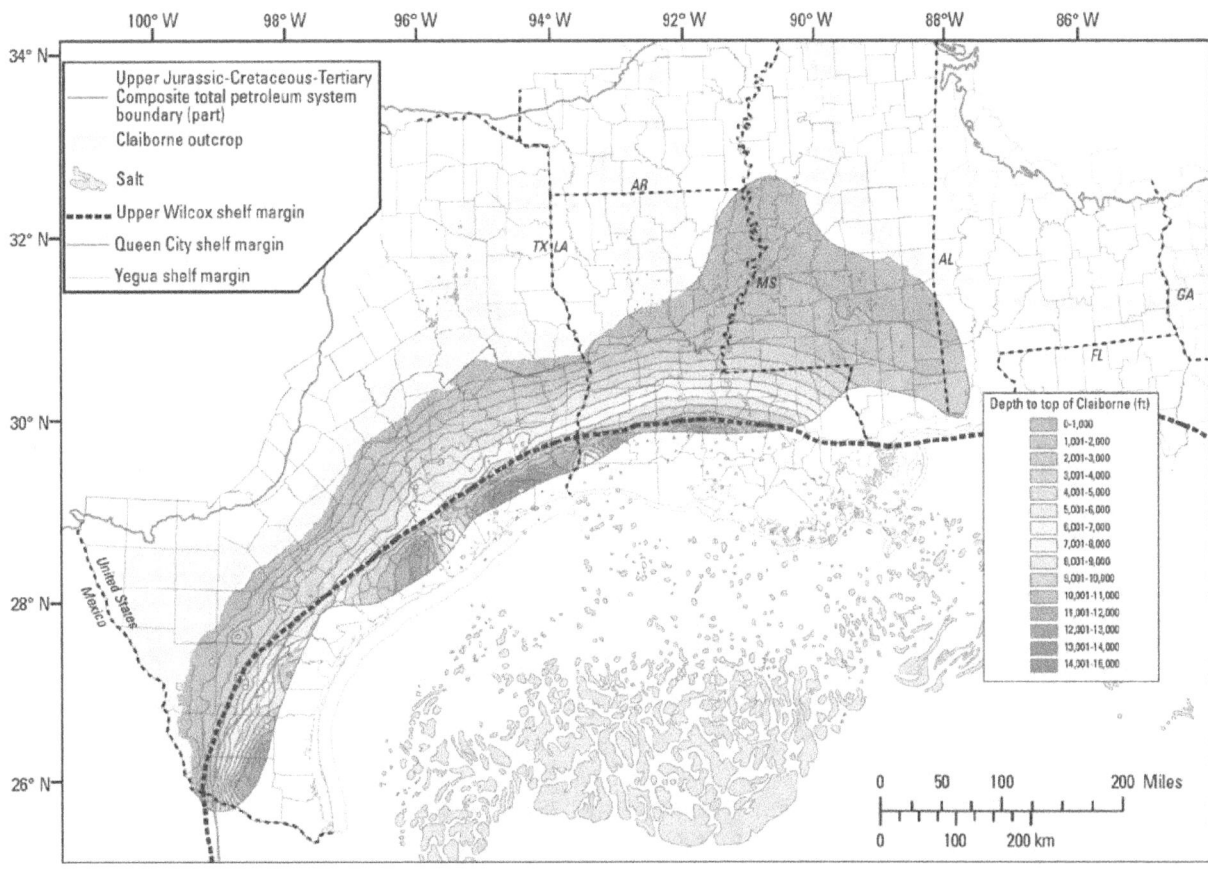

Figure 13. Depth to the top of Claiborne (Yegua Formation) constructed from the IHS Energy Group (2005b) database using data current through 2004 and from the Paleo-Data, Inc. (1989) Tenroc Regional Geologic database. Tops data from IHS Energy Group (2005b) were combined with paleontologic data from Paleo-Data, Inc. (1989) in ArcMap 9.1 (Environmental Systems Research Institute, Inc), and a kriging process was used to create a surface grid for formation tops. The top surface grid was subtracted from the elevation at surface to create the depth-to-top grid. The Claiborne Group outcrop is from Schruben and others (1994); salt is from Ewing and Lopez (1991); shelf margins are from Galloway and others (2000). Insufficient tops data are available in the IHS and Tenroc databases east of the Mississippi-Alabama State boundary to extend the Claiborne Group isopach farther eastward confidently.

the assessment of the Wilcox Group (Warwick and others, 2007), primarily because it cannot be separated from the Wilcox Group in the subsurface based on lithology alone.

Overlying the basal shales of the Reklaw Formation (called Bigford Formation near the outcrop in south Texas) is the Queen City Sand (Kennedy, 1892), an important hydrocarbon reservoir in south Texas and across the border into the Burgos Basin of northeastern Mexico. The Queen City Sand is described as transitional with the underlying Reklaw Formation (Ramos and Galloway, 1990) and is disconformably overlain by transgressive shelf muds of the Weches Formation. The Queen City Sand is present only as far northeast as the Texas-Louisiana border (Guevara and García, 1972). The name Mount Selman Formation also was used as a Queen City Sand equivalent in Texas (Kennedy, 1892; Trowbridge, 1932) but is no longer in use. The name El Pico Clay was applied by Eargle (1968) to lignitic claystones of the Queen City Sand interval in

17

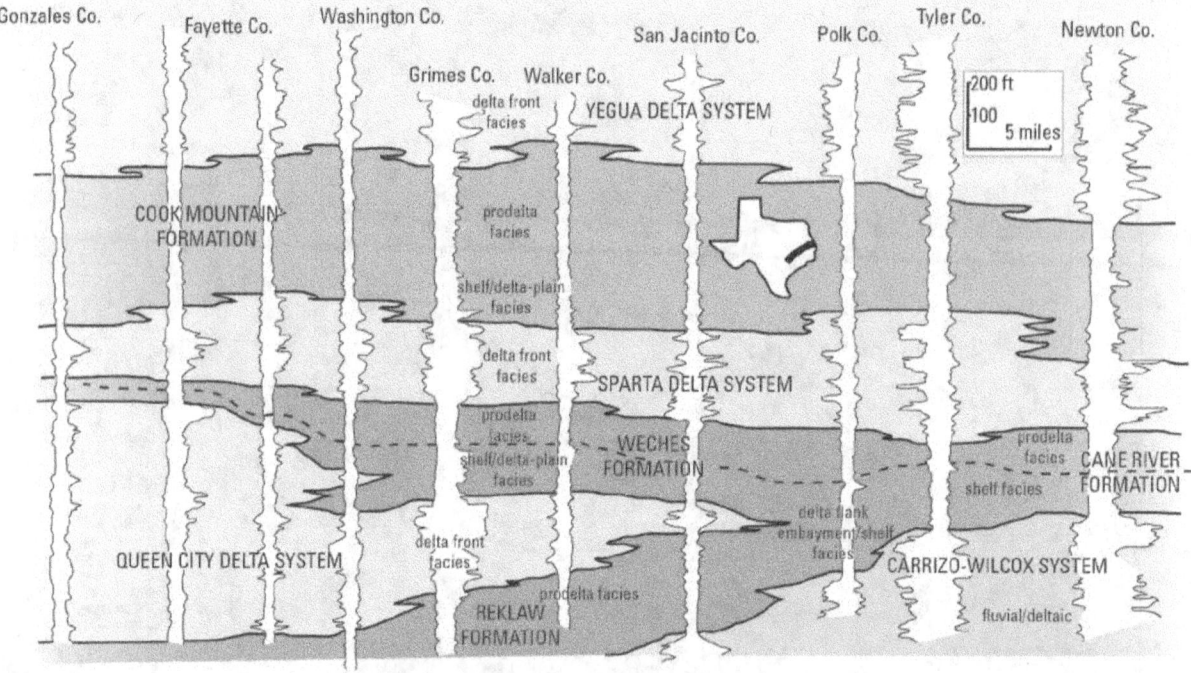

West   East

Figure 14. Spontaneous potential and resistivity log response of the lower Claiborne section in eastern Texas illustrating eastward loss of the Queen City Sand (from Ricoy and Brown (1977); see Ricoy (1976) for original data). Dashed line illustrates division between prodelta and shelf/delta-plain facies. Co. = County.

south Texas. Overlying the Queen City Sand in Texas are mudstones of the regional transgressive Weches Formation. The entire lower Claiborne section thins eastward into Louisiana, where the Queen City Sand is absent and the time-equivalent Cane River Formation comprises marl and distal shelf shales (fig. 14). Due to the width of the lower Claiborne shelf and the great distance from contemporary primary sediment supply on the Rio Grande Embayment axis, the Cane River Formation is less than 30 ft thick in some places in the subsurface in southern Louisiana(Vincent and Ewing, 2000). Vincent and Ewing (2000) described the regional-scale, log-based stratigraphic architecture of the lower Claiborne from southeast Texas through east-central Louisiana, demonstrating a pattern of low-angle, sigmoidal, clinoform downlaps separated by regional flooding surfaces. Lower Claiborne units prograded across the narrower shelf in south and central Texas out into slope environments. However, because of distance from sediment supply and a wider shelf in Louisiana, the lower Claiborne strata thin, downlap, and condense toward the east, where marl of the Cane River Formation rests by regional disconformity on the upper Wilcox Group (Vincent and Ewing, 2000).

The middle section of the Claiborne Group in Texas and Louisiana is composed of the hydrocarbon-bearing, progradational Sparta Sand (Spooner, 1926) and the overlying Cook Mountain Formation (Kennedy, 1892), which consists of glauconitic marine shale and marl at outcrop (Ewing, 1994). The name Crockett Formation (Stenzel, 1939) locally was used as an equivalent to the Cook Mountain Formation. The Sparta Sand is present throughout the Gulf Coast of Texas and Louisiana; however, most Sparta hydrocarbon production is from northern Louisiana. The thickness of the Sparta Sand is less than 700 ft in all of Texas (Ricoy and Brown, 1977). In south Texas, the Cook Mountain Formation is reported to have considerably different character than in east Texas (Gardner, 1938; Patterson, 1942; Eargle, 1968), where it is composed of 350 to 450 ft of chocolate brown and gray clay (Wendlandt and Knebel, 1926). In south Texas and into Mexico, the Cook Mountain Formation is described as consisting chiefly of glauconitic sands and sandstone (Trowbridge, 1932; Kane and Gierhart, 1935).

Ewing (1994) presented a discussion of "the Cook Mountain problem," which can be summarized as a historical inconsistency as to what constitutes this unit in the subsurface. At outcrop, the Cook Mountain Formation is a "diverse assemblage of marine-shelf and marginal marine environments associated with the maximum transgression between Sparta and Yegua prograding delta complexes" (Ewing, 1994, p. 227), that is, an easily recognized regional boundary between middle and upper Claiborne nonmarine sandy units, the Sparta Sand and the Yegua Formation, respectively. However, in the downdip subsurface, the overlying Yegua Formation becomes marginally marine and contains *Ceratobulimina eximia* in its lower portions, the first occurrence of which traditionally is used to designate Cook Mountain Formation in the updip subsurface. Therefore, the precise division between the Cook Mountain and Yegua Formations becomes uncertain in the downdip subsurface. In practical terms, this biostratigraphic pick results in the misidentification of Yegua Formation sand reservoirs, which yield *Ceratobulimina* as "Cook Mountain" in the NRG Associates (2006) database, and precludes a separate analysis of middle and upper Claiborne petroleum geology based on the NRG Associates (2006) data. The problem is well illustrated in figure 6 of Ewing (1994), reproduced here as figure 15. Figure 15 shows three ways to identify the Cook Mountain Formation: (1) as a genetic unit, including strata deposited in the time intervening between deposition of the Sparta Sand and the Yegua Formation, (2) as a lithostratigraphic unit, including facies identified as Cook Mountain at and near the outcrop, and (3) as a biostratigraphic unit including all *Ceratobulimina*-bearing strata in the subsurface. In part, because Cook Mountain and Yegua Formation reservoirs are inseparable in the NRG Associates (2006) database, the Claiborne was divided into Lower (primarily Queen City Sand), and Upper (Sparta Sand, Yegua and Cook Mountain Formations) AUs for this assessment, rather than Lower, Middle, and Upper AUs, as the stratigraphic division would have it.

The upper Claiborne section is composed of the sand-rich Yegua Formation across Texas, which is equivalent to the Cockfield Formation in Louisiana and Mississippi (Mancini and Tew, 1994; Johnston and others, 2000). The upper Claiborne section is referred to as the Gosport Sand in Alabama (Mancini and Tew, 1994). Some workers consider the uppermost sands in the Texas Yegua Formation as an informal "Cockfield Zone" (Hardin and Clark, 1968), on the basis of the presence of the foraminifera *Nonionella cockfieldensis*. Persistent strike-elongate sand lenses in the upper Yegua Formation of south Texas have been given informal and local names including the Bruni, O'Hern, Pettus, and Rosenburg Sands (West, 1963). These local sand names sometimes are used to code the producing formation in the NRG Associates (2006) database, resulting in multiple formation codes for upper Claiborne Yegua Formation oil and gas production. Ewing (2008) described the lower Yegua Formation of south Texas as a strandplain system and upper Yegua Formation strata as a barrier bar system pinching out updip into lagoonal facies. Davies and Ethridge (1971) reported that the south Texas Yegua Formation outcrop principally is composed of claystones, with thin limestones and sandstones. In central Texas, the Yegua Formation comprises almost one-half of the thickness of the Claiborne Group at outcrop, where it is 1,100 ft thick (Davies and Ethridge, 1971). Ewing and Vincent (1997a) presented a regional correlation of Yegua and Cockfield Formation strata from Texas into Louisiana. An important observation made by these workers is that the lower Yegua Formation cycles lose sand eastward and condense into a

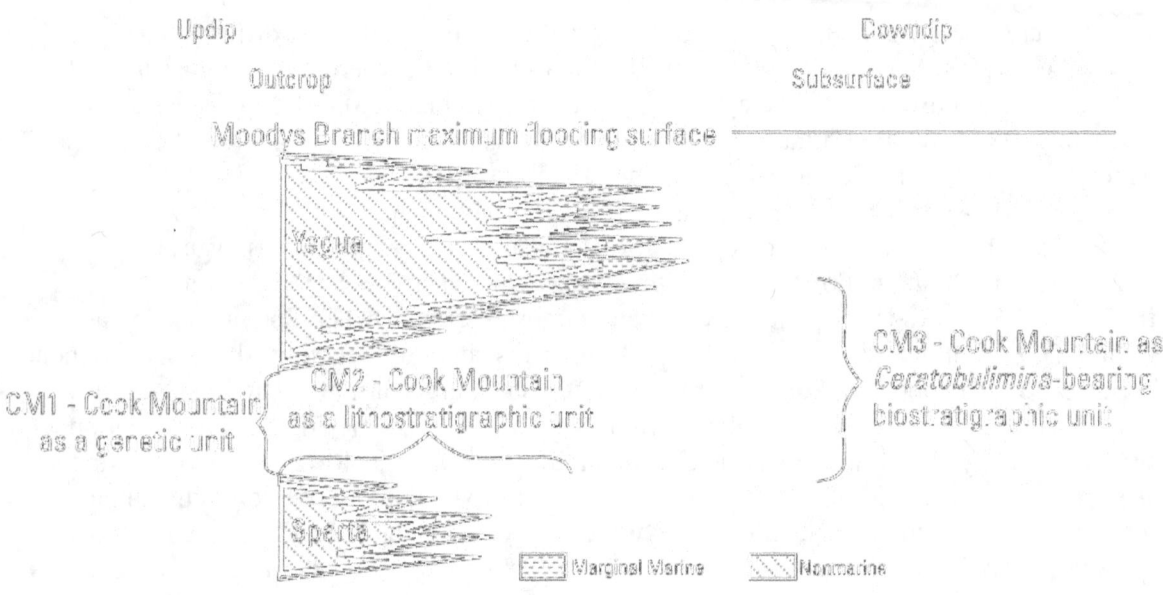

Figure 15. Graphic representation of the Cook Mountain problem. The Cook Mountain Formation is shown as (1) CM1 – a genetic unit, time-correlative with the outcrop Cook Mountain; (2) CM2 – a lithostratigraphic unit, representing the formally defined Cook Mountain Formation; and (3) a biostratigraphic unit, representing *Ceratobulimina*-bearing strata time-correlative with outcropping Cook Mountain and lower Yegua Formation (from Ewing, 1994). See text for additional explanation.

thin (<100 ft thick) marly shale unit called the "Sparta Lime" (not equivalent to the underlying Sparta Sand).

The Claiborne Group is overlain by the regionally transgressive Moodys Branch Marl of the lowermost Jackson Group (Cooke, 1918). The thin (10–100 ft) Moodys Branch Marl primarily consists of marine glauconitic sands and marl (Tew, 1992) and represents Upper Eocene sea level transgression across a maximum flooding surface following deposition of the sand-rich upper Claiborne Group (Galloway and others, 2000).

Paleogeography, Sediment Source Areas, and Depositional Systems

Following deposition of the mostly fluvial Carrizo Sand during the Early Eocene, regional transgressive shelf muds of the Reklaw Formation blanketed the northwest Gulf of Mexico margin beginning at about 49 Ma (Galloway and others, 2000). This period of sea level transgression and sediment starvation in the northern Gulf of Mexico records a temporary cessation of major uplift in the southern Rocky Mountains and Sierra Madre. These conditions persisted for the remainder of the Middle-Late Eocene during Claiborne Group deposition, interrupted by periodic pulses of brief, rejuvenated sediment input (Galloway, 2005). Local sandstones in the transgressive Reklaw Formation are glauconitic, in contrast to the underlying nonmarine Carrizo Sand, which locally contains interbedded lignites (Shellman, 1985). Subsidence in the Gulf of Mexico Basin primarily was load driven rather than tectonic; therefore, changes in relative sea level were a result of eustatic fluctuations, assuming that compaction remained relatively constant (Winker, 1982; Galloway and Williams, 1991).

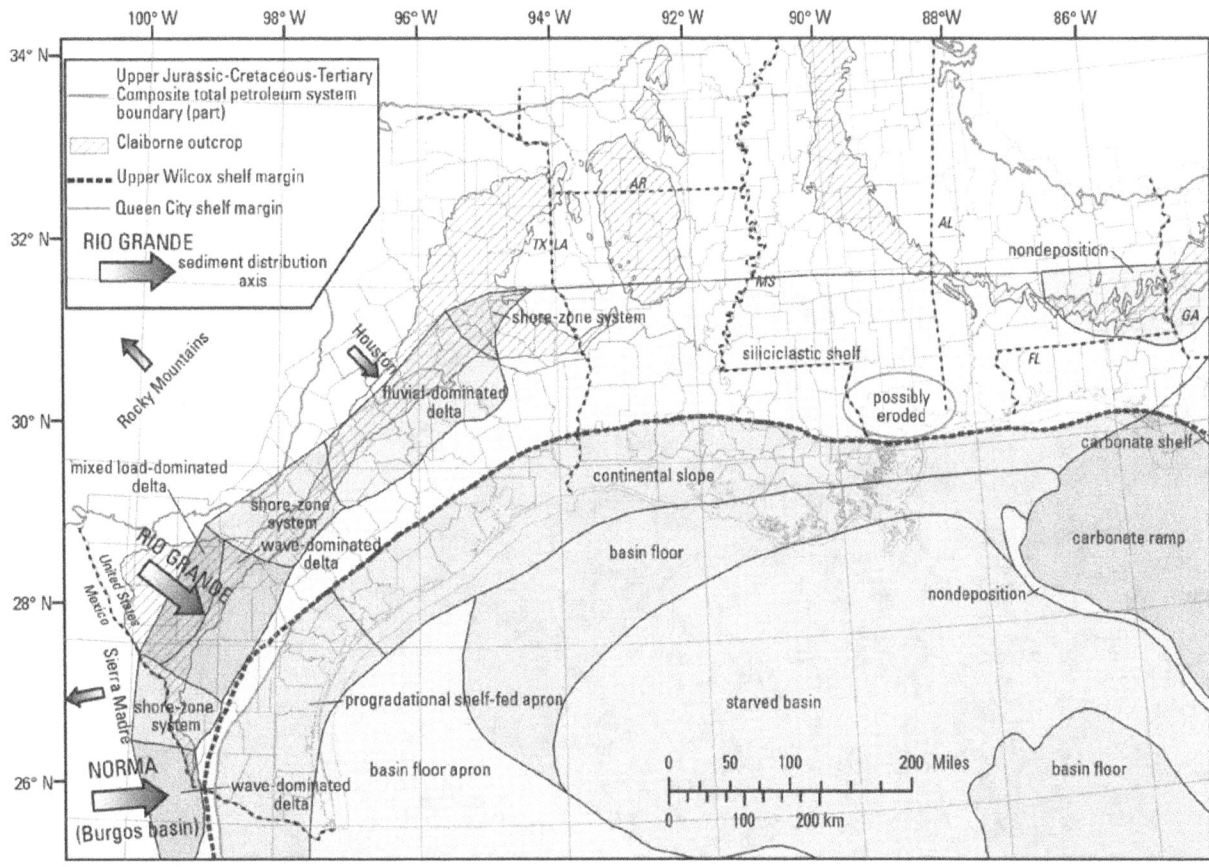

Figure 16.   Depositional systems of the lower Claiborne Group (from Galloway and others, 2000). Claiborne outcrop is from Schruben and others (1994). Possible erosion of Claiborne in Mississippi is from O'Donnell (1974) and Dockery (1976).

Recording a pulse of Laramide uplift in the Sierra Madre, deposition of the lower Claiborne Queen City Sand was focused into the Rio Grande Embayment and Norma depositional axes (fig. 16), where wave-dominated platform delta systems prograded into the Gulf of Mexico. Prodelta muds from the Norma and the Rio Grande Embayment axes prograded over the northwest margin as much as 20 miles (mi) locally (Galloway and others, 2000). In addition, rapid creation of accommodation space on the shelf allowed for the growth of inner-shelf deltas and some sediment deposition far landward of the contemporary shelf margin (Galloway and Williams, 1991). To the northeast of the primary sediment focus in southern Texas, a smaller, lobate, fluvial-dominated Houston delta system was present in southeastern Texas (Galloway and others, 2000). Into Louisiana and to the east, a muddy shelf covered the entire north-central basin area, represented by the condensed Cane River Formation of Louisiana. Claiborne Group deposition did not advance the shelf margin appreciably over the underlying upper Wilcox Group shelf break in Louisiana. Overlying the Queen City Sand, condensed, glauconitic shales of the Weches Formation record primarily marine deposition at the lower-middle Claiborne transition during a period of regional transgressive flooding. This interval marks an extended period of low sediment influx and the lapse of uplift in the western continent (Galloway and others, 2000).

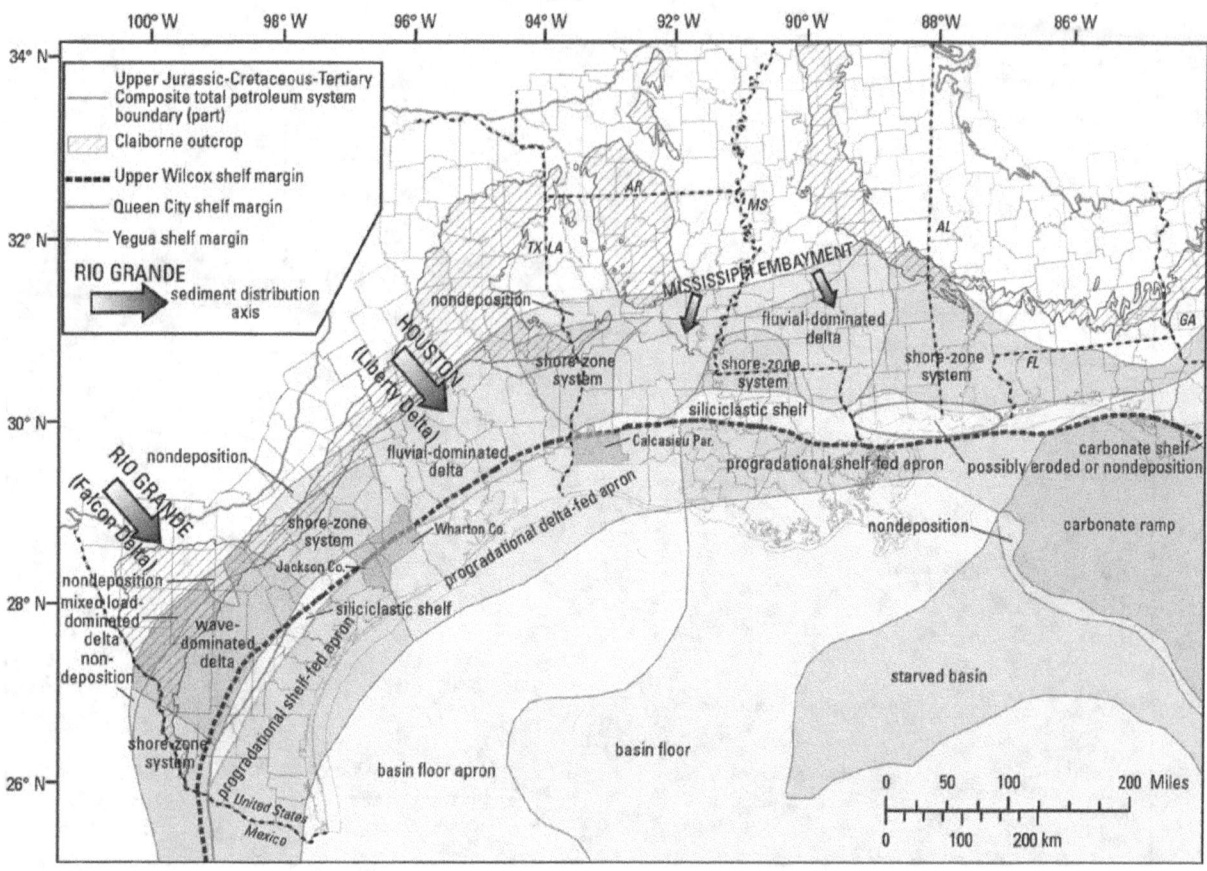

Figure 17. Depositional systems of the upper Claiborne Group (from Galloway and others, 2000). Claiborne outcrop is from Schruben and others (1994). Possible erosion/nondeposition of Claiborne in Mississippi and Alabama is from O'Donnell (1974) and Dockery (1976).

During approximately 44–40 Ma, the Sparta Sand was deposited in the north-central part of the basin primarily along the Mississippi Embayment axis, the dominant axis of sediment input during this period. Sparta Sand deposition was platform restricted and occurred far landward of the contemporary shelf edge. As a result, Middle Claiborne Group deposition did not appreciably advance the shelf margin over the earlier Queen City Sand, leaving the outer shelf relatively sediment starved (Galloway and Williams, 1991).

The upper Claiborne Group depositional episode from approximately 40–37 Ma occurred as a result of renewed uplift in the Mexican Cordillera. Deposition of the Yegua Formation caused basinward migration of the shelf edge throughout Texas. The Liberty Delta complex in the Houston Embayment and the Falcon Delta in the Rio Grande Embayment axis were the primary points of sediment dispersal (fig. 17). The rapid progradation of the Liberty Delta and accumulation of sediment at the shelf margin resulted in subregional mass wasting and subsequent deposition of reservoir sandstones far downdip of the shelf margin (Edwards, 1991; Hull, 1995; Ewing and Vincent, 1997b; Swenson, 1997; Galloway and others, 2000).

Elements of the Petroleum System

The Gulf of Mexico Basin is one of the world's most important petroleum provinces (Nehring, 1991). As such, diverse research has been directed at understanding the generation, migration, and trapping of its hydrocarbon resources (Koons and others, 1974; Laplante, 1974; Nunn and Sassen, 1986; Evans, 1987; Walters and Dusang, 1988; Sassen and others, 1988; Sassen and Moore, 1988; Sassen, 1990; Thompson and others, 1990; Price, 1991; Gregory and others, 1991; McDade and others, 1993; Zimmerman and Sassen, 1993; Echols and others, 1994; Wagner and others, 1994; Wenger and others, 1994; Wescott and Hood, 1994; Losh, 1998; Zimmerman, 1999; Nelson and others, 2000; Fillon, 2001; Gatenby, 2001; Hood and others, 2002; Lewan, 2002; Cathles, 2004, Mancini and others, 2006, among many others). Collectively, these workers have demonstrated that Gulf of Mexico Basin hydrocarbons are sourced from a number of stratigraphic intervals, including the Oxfordian Smackover Formation and Kimmeridgian-Tithonian Bossier Shale and Haynesville Formation (Jurassic), possibly the Aptian Pearsall Formation (Lower Cretaceous), the Turonian Eagle Ford Formation (Upper Cretaceous), and the Thanetian-Ypresian Wilcox Group and Sparta Sand (Tertiary) (fig. 2).

Organic matter maturation and the generation and migration of hydrocarbon resources from a particular source interval are dependent on location within the Gulf Basin. Most reservoired Claiborne hydrocarbons are interpreted to be sourced from the lower Tertiary section (fig. 18; McDade and others, 1993; Hood and others, 2002). As described earlier, the conventional hydrocarbon resources contained in the approximately 700 known Claiborne Group reservoirs across the study area are considered to be part of the Upper Jurassic-Cretaceous-Tertiary Composite total petroleum system that was defined for this assessment (fig. 3). Ideas regarding elements of the Upper Jurassic-Cretaceous-Tertiary Composite total petroleum system, including the timing of generation and accumulation of hydrocarbons in the Claiborne Group, are summarized in the events chart presented in figure 19.

Source Rocks and Thermal Maturation

Strong evidence directly linking the charge of Claiborne oil reservoirs to a particular source interval is lacking due to the relative infrequency of Tertiary source rock penetrations in the Gulf Coast. However, several authors have postulated that the downdip, deeply buried marine portions of the Paleocene-Eocene Wilcox and Claiborne groups could potentially be good source rock candidates of appropriate maturity for oil and gas generation (Schenk and Viger, 1996a, b; Sassen and others, 1988; Sassen, 1990). Thermal maturity of the Paleogene section would be enhanced by deep burial under the Miocene-Pleistocene in southern Louisiana, where McDade and others (1993) reported that the top of the Claiborne Group rapidly deepens basinward from 9,000 to 17,500 ft over the Cretaceous-Wilcox shelf edge. Work by Zimmerman (2000) indicated that the Eocene section was covered by >30,000 ft of Neogene sediments for much of coastal Louisiana and was buried to more than 35,000 ft in southeastern coastal Louisiana. In fact, Zimmerman (2000) predicted that thermal destruction of Eocene-hosted hydrocarbons was occurring throughout much of southern Louisiana (south of the Cretaceous-Wilcox shelf edge) due to hostile burial conditions at depths greater than about 27,000 ft. Warwick (2006) constructed a present-day thermal maturity map for the top of the Wilcox, based on vitrinite reflectance data, illustrating that the Paleogene is thermally mature for hydrocarbon generation across much of the northern Gulf Basin nearing the present-day coastline (fig. 20). Additional information on the modeling of Wilcox thermal maturation has been presented by Rowan and others (2007).

23

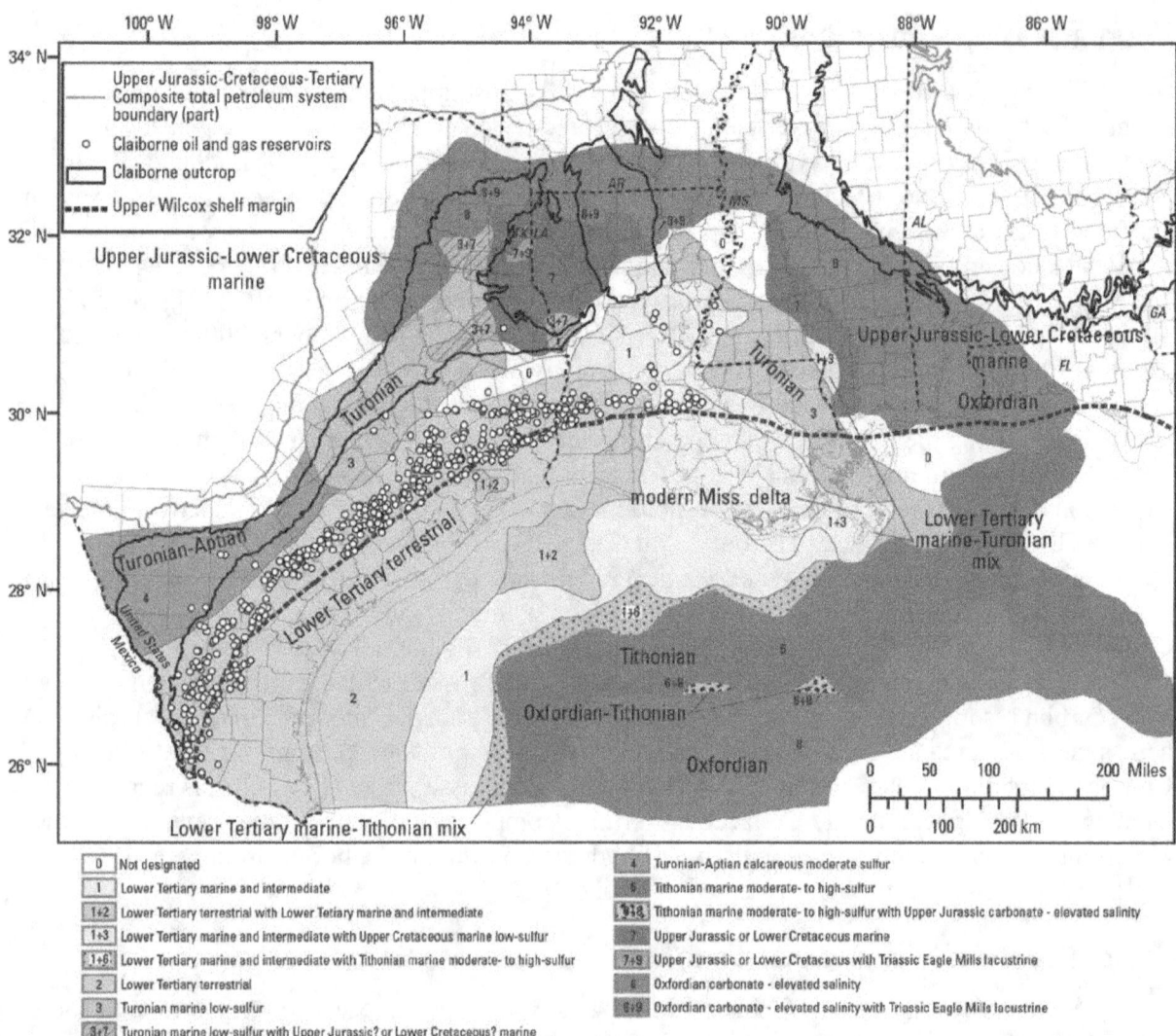

Figure 18. Hydrocarbon families of the U.S. Gulf Coast (from Hood and others, 2002). Claiborne Group outcrop is from Schruben and others (1994); Wilcox Group shelf margin is from Galloway and others (2000). This diagram shows families of reservoired oil and gas that originated from common source rocks, as compared to figure 3, which shows the boundary of the Upper Jurassic-Cretaceous-Tertiary Composite total petroleum system that was defined for this assessment. Miss. = Mississippi. The uncolored areas in the figure were not assigned to a hydrocarbon family in Hood and others (2002).

Characterization of crude oils from Wilcox and older Tuscaloosa and Smackover reservoirs in Louisiana and Mississippi illustrates that the oils contained in the younger reservoirs are geochemically distinct from those reservoired in the older reservoirs (Sassen and others, 1988). In particular, workers in Louisiana have demonstrated oil-source rock correlations using the biomarker 18α-oleanane (not present in crude oils from Mesozoic sources), confirming that oils sourced from Wilcox-Sparta strata have charged Wilcox reservoirs in south Louisiana (Walters and Dusang, 1988; McDade and others, 1993).

The Paleocene-Eocene Wilcox and Sparta contain mostly terrestrial gas-prone kerogen in the updip environment in central Louisiana and southwest Mississippi and only become more oil

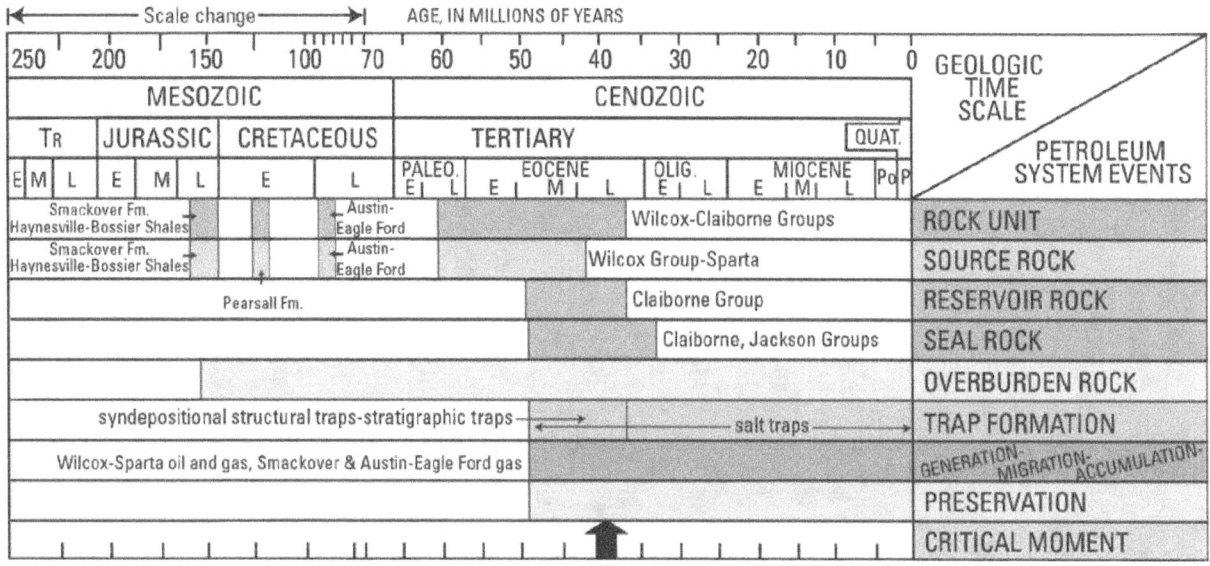

Figure 19. Events chart summarizing the major elements of the Upper Jurassic-Cretaceous-Tertiary Composite total petroleum system of the Gulf Basin (modified from Condon and Dyman, 2006). The critical moment is defined as the point in time that best represents the generation, migration, and accumulation of most of the hydrocarbons in the Upper Jurassic-Cretaceous-Tertiary Composite total petroleum system. As relates to the Claiborne Group, this is in the latter part of the Middle Eocene when the sand-rich Yegua and Cockfield reservoirs were deposited. E = Early, M = Middle, L = Late, T$_R$ = Triassic, Paleo. = Paleocene, Olig. = Oligocene, Po = Pliocene, P = Pleistocene, Quat. = Quaternary.

prone downdip (Sassen and others, 1988; Gregory and others, 1991). McDade and others (1993) reported mixed terrestrial and marine organic matter (Type II/III mixed kerogen) with low hydrogen indices of about 100 milligrams hydrocarbon per gram (mg HC/g) of total organic carbon (TOC) for >90 percent of 1,100 lower Tertiary marine shales from south Louisiana collected from depths of 9,000 to 16,000 ft. TOC contents for these samples were in the range 0.5 to 2.0 percent. The remainder of their samples (McDade and others, 1993) ranged to as high as 6.0 percent TOC and contained more oil-prone Type II organic matter with hydrogen indices of 200 mg HC/g TOC or more. Gregory and others (1991) reported a modest correlation between fluorescence intensity and hydrogen index for Sparta and Wilcox samples and concluded that the organic material was dominantly terrestrial Type III but was deposited in a marine environment. Gregory and others (1991) reported that Sparta samples were thermally immature and Wilcox Group samples were thermally mature for oil generation. Hood and others (2002) suggested that regional differences in the types of lower Tertiary organic matter deposited in the Gulf Basin were responsible for variations in the distribution of oil versus gas. In particular, Hood and others (2002) pointed out that more marine Type II source rocks in Louisiana appeared to produce a greater proportion of oil, whereas terrestrially sourced organic matter produced more gas-prone hydrocarbons in Texas (fig. 18).

Analyses of sidewall cores collected from a deep offshore well drilled east of the modern Mississippi delta revealed good source rock potential for thermally immature lower Tertiary strata (Wagner and others, 1994). Samples from the lower Tertiary had TOC contents of 0.9 to 3.3 percent with some hydrogen indices >500, indicative of a marine Type II kerogen (Wagner and others, 1994). The authors concluded that lithologies similar to those drilled could be thermally

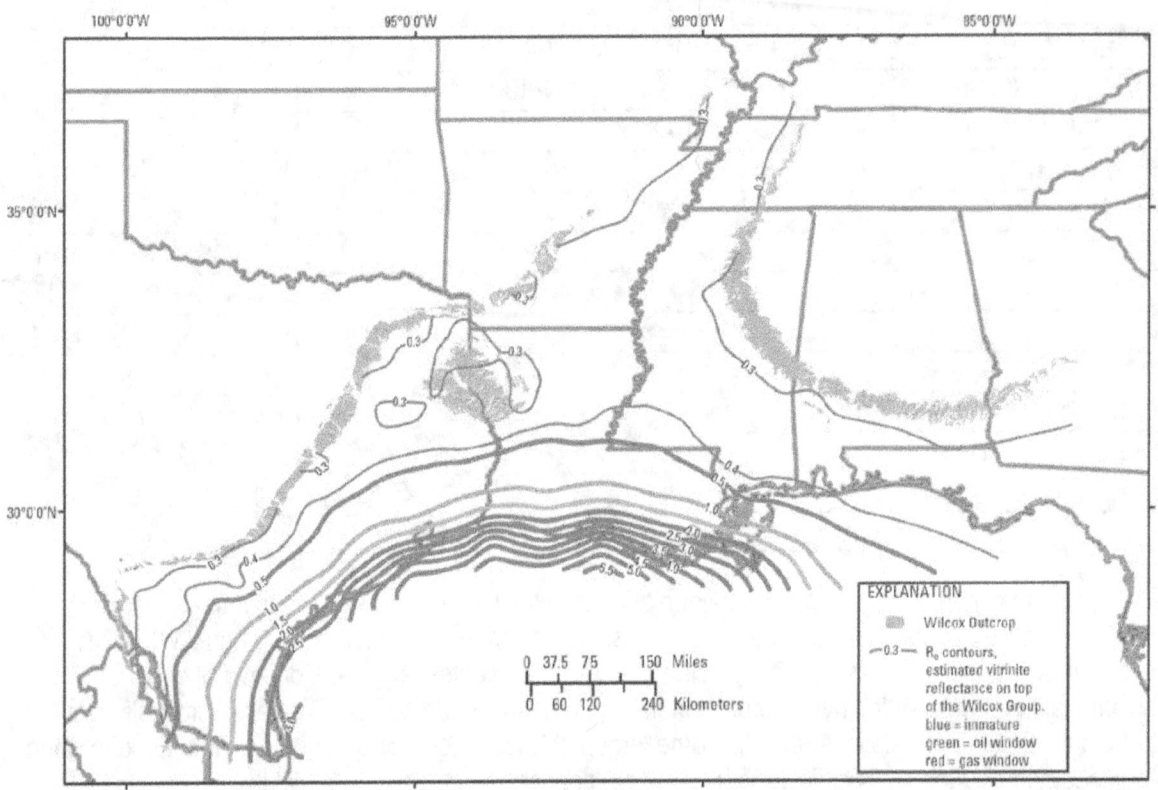

Figure 20. Present-day thermal maturity of the top of the Wilcox Group (from Warwick, 2006). Claiborne outcrop is from Schruben and others (1994); Wilcox Group shelf margin is from Galloway and others (2000).

mature for oil generation locally due to shallower water depths, increased overburden thickness, and higher heat flow. A one-dimensional (1-D) burial history model for southern Louisiana indicates that Eocene source rocks entered the oil window at 25.7 Ma (Oligocene), reached peak oil generation at 14.9 Ma (middle Miocene), and entered the wet gas window in the late Miocene 7.3 Ma (Nelson and others, 2000). Thermal history modeling by McDade and others (1993) also indicated that the Paleogene section was thermally mature for oil generation in southwestern Louisiana and that Lower Cretaceous and Jurassic source rocks were overmature across southern Louisiana.

Some Tertiary-sourced oil (Hood and others, 2002) production from the Sparta Sand in northern Louisiana is far removed from the possible locations of thermally mature potential lower Tertiary source rocks, which would occur south of the Cretaceous shelf break (Sassen, 1990). In this case, very long range lateral migration must have occurred if the Sparta oils are indeed sourced by lower Tertiary rocks. Otherwise, vertical migration from Turonian and Tithonian source rocks may be a possibility in this area (Sassen, 1990).

Shellman (1985) suggested that shales in the Paleocene Midway Group may also be potential source rocks in the Tertiary Gulf of Mexico Basin; pyrolysis study of Midway samples from Mississippi and Louisiana by Sassen (1990) confirms moderate source potential. There do not appear to be any potential source rock intervals in the northern half of the Gulf of Mexico Basin higher in the section than the Lower Oligocene (Dow, 1977). This is due in part to the high rates of deposition, which limited the overall proportion of organic matter contained in the sediments, and the recent age of deposition, which limits thermal maturity (Nunn and Sassen, 1986; Nehring, 1991). In addition, despite predictions of good preservation potential for Type II kerogen in anoxic intraslope basins (Dow, 1984), studies of the type of organic matter contained in upper Tertiary strata indicate that most is of terrestrial origin with little potential for oil generation (Fang and others, 1989).

As part of the Gulf of Mexico assessment, a regional thermal maturation history of the Wilcox was reconstructed based on 1-D burial history models of 53 wells in the Texas Coastal Plain (Rowan and others, 2007). Their work indicated that the downdip portions of the basal Wilcox entered the oil window in the Early Eocene, and the maturation front has since gradually moved updip during deposition of Cenozoic overburden. At the present day, hydrocarbon generation is complete in the basal Wilcox but is ongoing farther updip. The farthest updip portions of the Wilcox, north of the Wilcox shelf margin, are undermature for hydrocarbon generation (Claypool and Mancini, 1989; Mancini and others, 1999, 2006; Warwick, 2006; Rowan and others, 2007).

Regional burial history modeling by Lewan (2002) in the onshore central Gulf Coast area (eastern Texas, Louisiana, southern Mississippi) demonstrated cracking of Smackover oil to gas beginning as long ago as 89 Ma in some locations and continuing to the present. Gas generated by cracking of Smackover oils could have charged Claiborne reservoirs from their deposition until present. According to the Lewan (2002) study, Turonian strata in southern Louisiana mostly are undermature for gas cracking; however, cracking of Turonian oil may charge gas to Claiborne reservoirs in the downdip portions of the basin. In the Lewan (2002) study, four locations at the downdip coastal portion of the study area indicated gas generation via cracking of Turonian oil.

Migration of Hydrocarbons

Migration of oil and gas in the Cenozoic Gulf of Mexico Basin dominantly is short-range vertical, occurring along the abundant growth faults associated with sediment deposition, or along faults associated with salt movement and emplacement (Nunn and Sassen, 1986; Sassen and others, 1988; Sassen, 1990; Nehring, 1991; Price, 1991; Schenk and Viger, 1996a, b; Losh, 1998). Migration of oil and gas from deep mature mudrocks probably also has occurred up stratal collapse zones created by salt evacuation (Hood and others, 2002). Dominantly vertical migration is responsible for the distribution of hydrocarbon families seen in the Hood and others (2002) study; in general, hydrocarbons from a particular source are reservoired above the areas where that source is mature. Lateral migration of up to 3 mi may also constitute an important migration pathway; medium distance or longer (> 30 mi) migration probably is rare (Nehring, 1991). However, Sassen and others (1988) and Sassen (1990) suggested long-range lateral migration (up to 100 mi) of Wilcox crude oils from mature downdip marine source facies was necessary to charge Wilcox reservoirs in central Louisiana (fig. 21). Wescott and Hood (1994) also invoked long-range lateral migration of hydrocarbons to charge reservoirs in the East Texas Salt Basin. As described above, migration and emplacement of Tertiary-sourced oils into Sparta Sand reservoirs of north-central Louisiana is best explained as a consequence of long-range lateral migration from thermally mature Tertiary sources south of the Cretaceous shelf break. Work by Cathles and colleagues (summarized in Cathles, 2004) demonstrated that a high volume of the hydrocarbons currently being generated in the deep Gulf of Mexico offshore source strata simply flow through the system and are expelled directly into the overlying waters, where they are evidenced as hydrocarbon seeps on the seafloor and slicks upon the water surface (Hood and others, 2002). The Cathles (2004) studies further

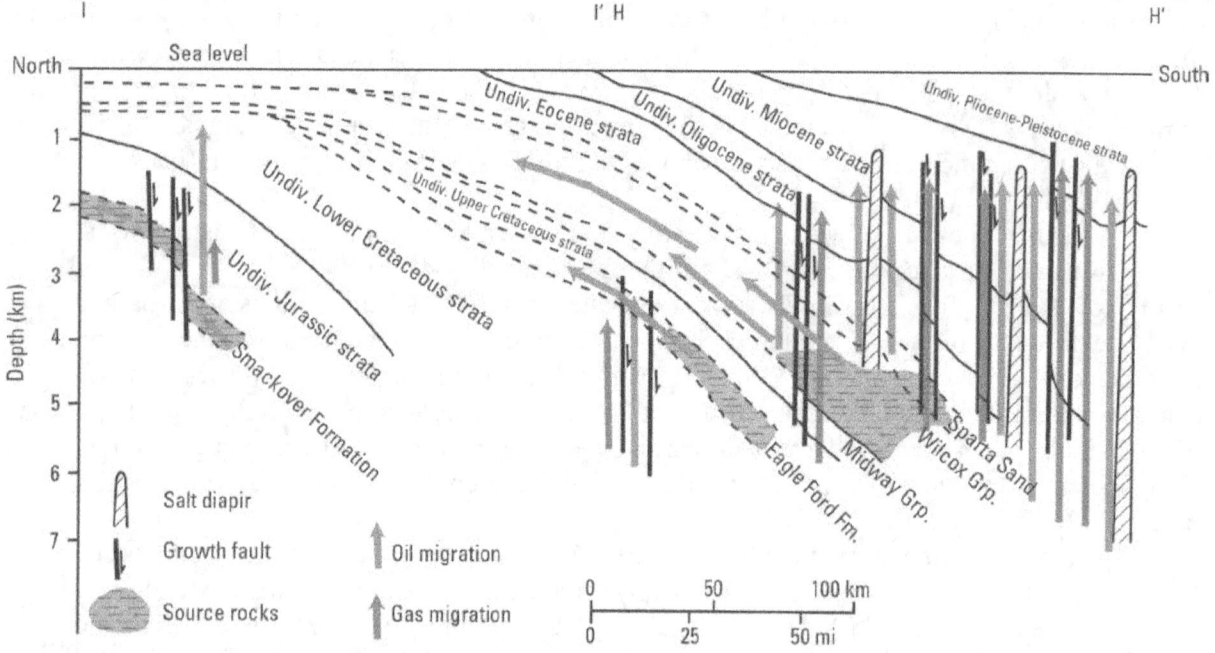

Figure 21. Conceptualized migration of oil and gas in southern Louisiana (from Sassen, 1990). Location of section is shown in figure 12. This cartoon cross section is based on the I-I' and H-H' cross sections constructed by Eversull (1984) and Bebout and Gutiérrez (1982), respectively. Grp. = Group, Fm. = Formation, Undiv. = undivided, km = kilometer.

demonstrated that offshore reservoirs are filling from the current and geologically recent flow-through patterns of hydrocarbon migration. In addition, Cathles (2004) observed the gas washing of oil, which occurred through the removal of *n*-alkanes. This characteristic may help to delineate the location of potential gas reservoirs in exploration by systematic analysis of oil compositions. Work by Gatenby (2001) empirically demonstrated that the largest oil and gas accumulations in the deepwater Gulf of Mexico offshore occur proximally above the depth at which gas and oil become cosoluble and that no commercial accumulations of oil occur below the depth at which oil and gas phase-separate. Gatenby (2001) also pointed out that the greater the magnitude of the vertical change of oil in gas solubility, the greater the size of the accumulation. This suggests that vertically migrating hydrocarbons are emplaced in response to changes in temperature and pressure conditions and explains the relationship between hydrocarbon pay and the top of overpressure in the Gulf of Mexico Basin (Leach, 1993).

Reservoir Rocks

Lower Claiborne - Queen City Sand and Reklaw Formation

The Queen City Sand is thickest in south Texas (fig. 22), where strike-oriented, coastal barrier reservoir sands accumulated as part of a highly destructive wave-dominated delta system (Guevara and García, 1972). Reservoir facies generally are downdip from the sand maxima and interfinger with prodelta muds. Lobate sand geometries in eastern Texas are interpreted to indicate a highly constructive delta system. Sandy facies of the Queen City pinch out eastward toward

28

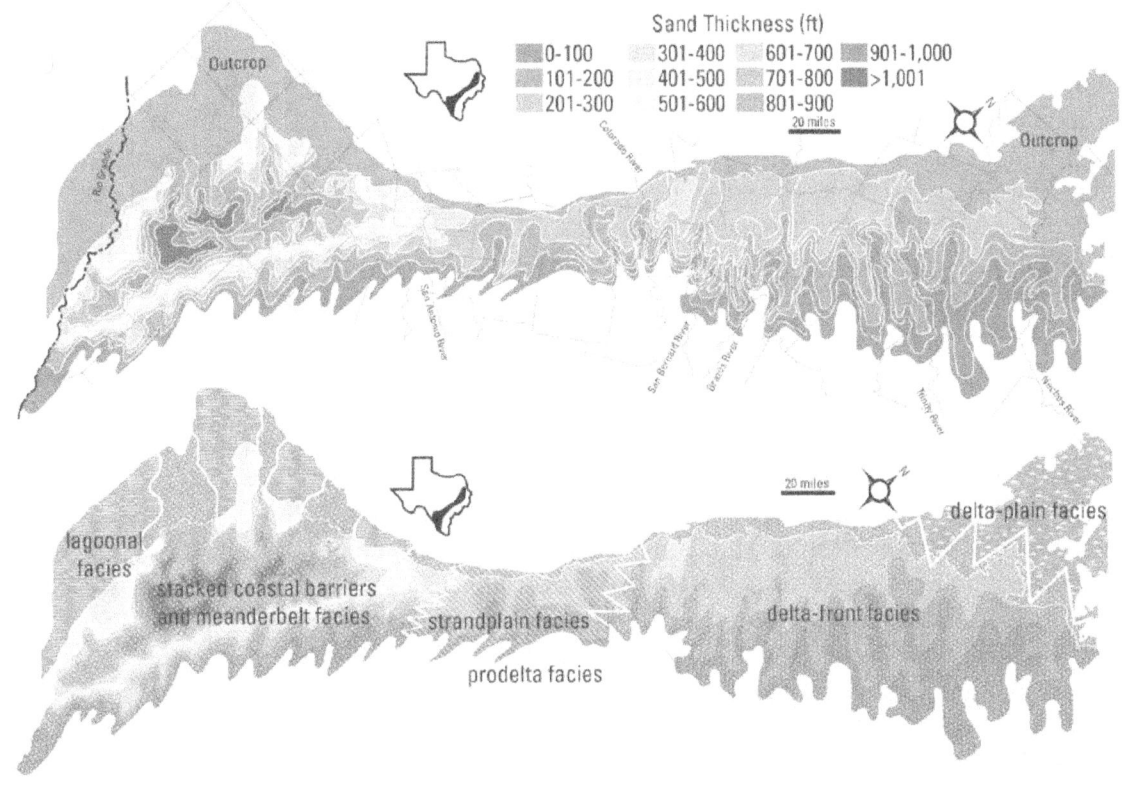

Figure 22. Sand isolith (top) and facies (bottom) map for the lower Claiborne Queen City Sand, Texas Coastal Plain (from Guevara and García, 1972).

Louisiana, where the overlying Weches Formation and underlying Reklaw Formation merge into the condensed Cane River marl (Guevara and García, 1972). Most of the updip fluvial facies of the Queen City were removed by erosion (Guevara and García, 1972). The Queen City is relatively unaffected by salt tectonics in the south Texas Rio Grande Embayment, as compared to upper Claiborne strata farther northeast in the salt-rich Houston Embayment. There are no Queen City reservoirs reported north of the San Marcos Arch (NRG Associates, 2006), although there are some producing wells listed north of the arch in the IHS database (IHS Energy Group, 2005b).

According to Galloway and Williams (1991), Queen City deposition did not build shelf-edge deltas; instead, inner-shelf delta sediments accumulated on the shelf platform far landward of the contemporary shelf edge. This was due to rapid creation of accommodation space by the subsidence of the shelf, possibly in a compensative response to fluvial bypass of the shelf by the upper Wilcox and loading of the shelf edge by upper Wilcox prograding deltas. In effect, this tectonic influence on deposition could reduce the potential for a downdip Queen City play. Since the bulk of Queen City sediments accumulated landward of the shelf margin, the inference is that no sands were transported into slope, basin floor, and other distal environments by the foundering or subsidence of shelf edges, stormwater retreat, or lowstand fan deposition. However, the more regional approach used by Galloway and others (2000), with the inclusion of deeper wells, illustrated substantial advancement of the Queen City shelf margin, implying significant transport of sandy sediments to the shelf edge and beyond (W.E. Galloway, The University of Texas at

Austin, written commun., 2006). Regardless, the current collective understanding among exploration geologists of the nature and location of the Queen City shelf margin in south Texas is considered poor at best (T.E. Ewing, Frontera Exploration Consultants, Inc., written commun., 2008).

Evaluation of the NRG Associates (2006) database indicates good reservoir quality for updip Queen City reservoirs, with reported average porosity ranging from 16 to 33 percent and reported average permeability ranging from 16 to 1,240 millidarcies (md). For the approximately 10 downdip Queen City reservoirs contained in the NRG Associates (2006) database, only one average porosity value of 19 md is reported, consistent with the range of 19 to 25 percent reported by Burnett (1990) for the Mestena Grande field (fig. 6) in southern Texas. Burnett (1990) reported that measured permeabilities typically ranged from 15 to 35 md at Mestena Grande, with a maximum reported value of 80 md.

Reservoirs generally are normally pressured in updip Queen City reservoirs, consistently following the Gulf of Mexico hydrostatic pressure line of 0.465 pounds per square inch per foot (psi/ft) (Dickinson, 1953). Schenk and Viger (1996a) reported that Queen City reservoirs are overpressured in more distal, downdip areas, consistent with the report by Burnett (1990) on the Mestena Grande field. Analysis of NRG Associates (2006) data indicates that all of the Queen City reservoirs in the downdip environment (8,000–12,000 ft) are overpressured (>5,000 psi).

Shellman (1985) described Reklaw Formation oil fields in Fayette, Gonzales, Wilson, and Atacosa Counties, Tex., where oil is produced from transgressive shoreline sands deposited as the Reklaw sea advanced over the coastal plain. Sams (1990) presented a sequence stratigraphic analysis of the Reklaw transgression in the same general geographic area. Oil-charged reservoirs with local names including the Mackhank, Luling, Slick, and Second and First Reklaw/Atkinson Sands (Sams, 1990) are at depths of 1,800 to 2,200 ft (Shellman, 1985). Shellman (1985) described this trend as composed of better quality sandstones to the northeast, with poorly developed and discontinuous sands to the southwest. In the Elm Grove field of Fayette County (fig. 6), Shellman (1985) described six 5- to 50-ft-thick reservoir intervals, separated by impermeable shales 2 to 15 ft thick. Reklaw sandstones have average porosity of 26 percent and permeability of <10 to 900 md (Shellman, 1985). Isolated clean sand lenses may have higher porosity and permeability; conversely, shaley laminations may negatively impact reservoir character. Compaction in transgressive Reklaw sandstones does not significantly impact porosity because of the shallow burial depths (Shellman, 1985). Composition of transgressive Reklaw sands is 60 percent fine-grained monocrystalline quartz, with a pore throat diameter of 70 micrometers (μm) (Shellman, 1985). Clays comprise 22 percent of the textural framework, and clay migration is believed to contribute to production problems (Shellman, 1985).

Middle Claiborne – Sparta Sand and Cook Mountain Formation

Ricoy and Brown (1977) described the depositional systems of the Sparta Sand in Texas, where a highly constructive delta dominated in east Texas and a highly destructive delta system dominated in south Texas. Sediment dispersal by fluvial processes was in the direction of dip in the highly constructive delta environment, and sandstone geometries generally are perpendicular to depositional strike with a lobate areal geometry. Facies recognized include delta plain distributary sandstones and interdistributary mudstones, delta-front sandstones, and prodelta mudstones. In central Texas, a strandplain-barrier bar system with sand geometries parallel to regional strike was built from sands transported longshore from the principal sediment input axes in south and east Texas. Well logs indicate that the Sparta Sand in Texas is a single sandstone unit with a maximum thickness of 100 ft, thinning downdip into shelf mud facies (Ricoy and Brown, 1977). In south Texas, the Sparta was deposited in a highly destructive delta system, characterized by sandstone maxima parallel to depositional strike, with a variety of depositional environments recognized, including coastal barrier sandstones, lagoonal mudstones, and prodelta and shelf mudstones (Ricoy and Brown, 1977). Sediment dispersal here and in the strandplain environment was parallel to strike. Galloway and Williams (1991) showed that Sparta accumulation rates were lower near the contemporary shelf edge, as compared to all other Gulf of Mexico Basin Cenozoic sequences, which had the highest accumulation rates near the shelf edge, decreasing landward.

Production from Sparta Sand reservoirs occurs in central Louisiana along the Mississippi Embayment axis (fig. 1), with several reservoirs scattered into central and south Texas. Nehring (1991) reported that Sparta reservoirs are at depths of 2,000 to 11,500 ft in Louisiana and are generally between 3 to 220 ft thick. Nehring (1991) reported that reservoir quality is good, with porosity generally ranging from 21 to 34 percent and permeability ranging from 60 to >1,000 md. This is consistent with the reservoir quality reported for the 11,500-ft-deep Fordoche oil field (fig. 6) in Point Coupee Parish (Krutak and Kimbrell, 1991). The absence of Sparta production in Texas is assumed to be the result of low sediment supply, which resulted in (1) thin prodelta muds, which would have acted as source beds, (2) a lack of growth faults to provide traps because of the thin delta front/prodelta facies, and (3) a lack of reservoirs of sufficient thickness compared to the overlying Yegua and the underlying Queen City Sand (Ricoy and Brown, 1977).

Cook Mountain reservoirs listed in the NRG Associates (2006) database are distributed evenly across central and east Texas, with a scattering (Crockett reservoirs) in south Texas. There are no Cook Mountain reservoirs reported in Louisiana in the NRG Associates (2006) database. Many of the Cook Mountain reservoirs and production wells (IHS Energy Group, 2005a) in Texas are on the Yegua trend (described below), suggesting that many may in fact be *Ceratobulimina*-bearing lower Yegua Formation sands (Ewing, 1994) rather than the glauconitic marine sands of the Cook Mountain, as described at outcrop in southern Texas by Trowbridge (1932) and Kane and Gierhart (1935).

Upper Claiborne – Yegua and Cockfield Formations

Depositional environments of the upper Claiborne Yegua and Cockfield Formations vary greatly, from fluvial to deltaic, strandplain, bar, and shelf and slope systems (Nehring, 1991; Ewing, 2008). Basinal reservoir facies also may be present below the depths of current drilling (T.E. Ewing, Frontera Exploration Consultants, Inc., written commun., 2008). In the high-constructive Liberty Delta system of the Houston Embayment, lobate, strike-normal delta front strata include thick sand-rich sequences vertically bounded by thin to thick marine muds (Fisher, 1969). In the south Texas Falcon delta, Yegua hydrocarbon reservoirs are an extensive strandline-barrier bar complex characterized by strike-parallel named sands including the Pettus, Rosenburg, Bruni, and O'Hern. The lower part of the Yegua primarily consists of strandplain facies, and the upper Yegua consists of barrier bar facies (Ewing, 2008). Fisher (1969) reported 800 to 1,000 ft of net sand in the upper Claiborne of south Texas and over 1,000 ft in the Houston Embayment (fig. 23).

The Yegua and Cockfield Formations are the only units in the Claiborne consistently reported to produce from a downdip shelf-slope facies. This probably is due to the high rate and volume of sediment input (Hull, 1995), which resulted in accumulation of sediments at the shelf margin, over-steepening of the upper slope, and the eventual foundering of the shelf edge, transporting reservoirs sands downdip (Edwards, 1991). In addition to catastrophic failure of the

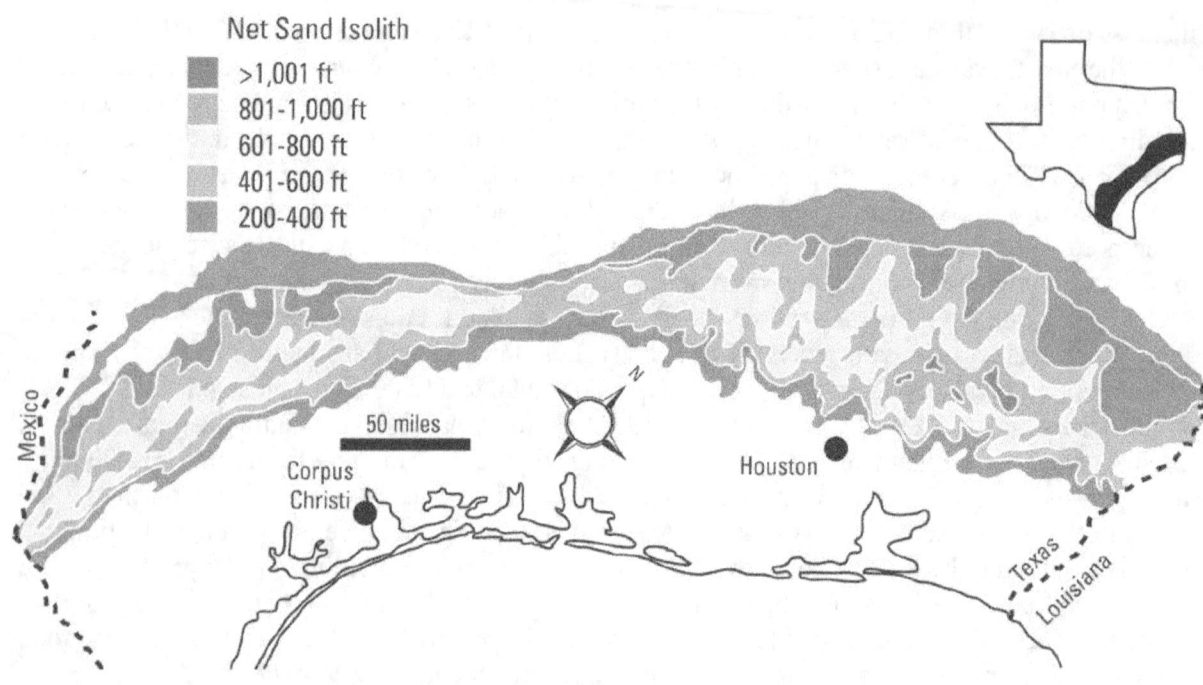

Figure 23. Sand isolith map for the upper Claiborne Yegua Formation, Texas Coastal Plain (from Fisher, 1969).

shelf edge, listric down-to-the-basin expansion-growth faults at the outer shelf and upper slope created significant accommodation space to receive sands in the downdip environment. Winker (1982) described the numerous stratigraphic and structural complexities that resulted from rapid expansion at the shelf margin, including large amounts of missing section due to faulting, marked deviations from the regional dip, the characteristic expansion across faults, and rapid facies changes. The resultant hydrocarbon reservoirs at and beyond the expanded and (or) foundered shelf edge are highly productive but not easy to predict (Ewing and Vincent, 1997b).

Fisher (1969) described the updip Yegua as composed of high-constructive delta systems characterized by multilateral fluvial sand units up to 200 ft thick, up to 30 mi in width, with thickness axes oriented normal to regional strike. According to Ewing (1994), the updip Yegua trend is more marine in character than the Yegua at outcrop but still contains a high proportion of fluvial channels and nonmarine shales. Downdip, sand reservoirs represent a number of environments, including channeled turbidite deposits on the outer shelf or upper slope, and thick strike-elongate sands interpreted as barrier bar complexes (Ewing and Fergeson, 1991). Miller (1993) reported that the shelf-margin downdip Yegua sandstones were deposited by gravity-flow mechanisms on a slope fan of a lowstand systems tract.

Whitten and Berg (1987) described 240 ft of downdip shaley sandstone Yegua core located about 20 mi basinward of thicker and more abundant fluvial Yegua sandstones in Jackson County, Tex. (fig. 17), as thin bedded, on average 2 ft, ranging 0.5 to 9 ft. Bioturbation was not present. Massive sandstones graded upward into thinly laminated to rippled sandstones to interlaminated sands and shales to complete the Bouma (1962) turbidite sequence. Whitten and Berg (1987) interpreted the sediment provenance to be the same as the overlying Oligocene Frio, on the basis of compositional similarities.

Lock and Voorhies (1988) reported that the downdip Yegua and Cockfield reservoirs in southwestern Louisiana typically have a laterally consistent log response, high shale-to-sand ratios, and contain relatively thin sands, all inconsistent with deposition in a deltaic setting and more likely characteristic of open-shelf facies. The sand bodies have geometries consistent with deposition by retreating storm surge waters. On the basis of their location, Lock and Voorhies (1988) interpreted the downdip Yegua and Cockfield sands to be of a shelf or deep-water origin deposited in a lowstand slope fan depositional environment.

Ewing and Fergeson (1991) reported on the structure and stratigraphy of downdip Yegua gas-condensate fields in Wharton County, Tex., where the reservoir intervals are enclosed in thick marine shales and are overlain by overpressured Jackson Group shales. Ewing and Fergeson (1991) described a highly variable stratigraphy in the downdip environment, where the sands are thick in some areas and absent in others.

Downdip Yegua reservoirs are overpressured (Whitten and Berg, 1987; Ewing and Fergeson, 1991). The Arco No. 1 Hoffpauir well in south-central Calcasieu Parish (fig. 17) penetrated 7,000 ft of overpressured shales before reaching downdip Yegua turbidite sands (Lock and Voorhies, 1988). The updip trend is normally pressured (Swenson, 1997).

Reservoir quality for Yegua sandstones is good to excellent, with porosity ranging from 10 to 38 percent and permeability from 20 to 3,000 md (Nehring, 1991). In south Texas, Yegua reservoirs have porosity of 23 to 33 percent and permeability of 40 to 800 md (Nehring, 1991, citing Galloway and others, 1983, and Kosters and others, 1989). Whitten and Berg (1987) reported that average porosity of downdip shaley sandstone Yegua core was 29 percent, and average permeability was 356 md in Jackson County, Tex. Miller (1993) reported slightly poorer reservoir quality, with average porosity at 16 percent and a permeability range of 1 to 20 md for deep Yegua sandstones deposited basinward of the shelf margin. Evaluation of the NRG Associates (2006) database indicates updip Yegua reservoirs have median porosity of 30 percent and median permeability of 400 md. Downdip reservoirs have slightly lower median porosity of 27 percent and median permeability of 175 md. Whitten and Berg (1987) interpreted intergranular secondary porosity as seen in thin sections of downdip Yegua sands to be a result both of dissolution of cements and of network detrital grains. Clays formed through diagenesis of feldspars are absent, interpreted to be a result of flushing from the overpressured hydraulics.

Traps and Seals

An evaluation of the NRG Associates (2006) database indicates that the traps containing Claiborne-reservoired hydrocarbon accumulations predominantly are described as structural, in most cases rollover anticlines downthrown to growth faults. Schenk and Viger (1996a) reported that lower Claiborne Queen City traps primarily are structural and occur on reactivated Wilcox growth faults and faulted anticlines. In the updip Claiborne depositional environment, many of the trapping faults may be reactivated older Wilcox growth faults. In the downdip Claiborne environment, the trapping faults are contemporary Claiborne growth faults (Ewing and Fergeson, 1991). An examination of the complex trapping structures created by growth faulting indicates that rollover anticlines, upthrown closures, and downthrown closures all play some role in trapping Claiborne hydrocarbon accumulations (fig. 24). Syndepositional growth faulting would have generated hydrocarbon traps since the beginning of Claiborne deposition, as hydrocarbon generation from underlying strata was ongoing. (See earlier section "Source Rocks and Thermal Maturation.")

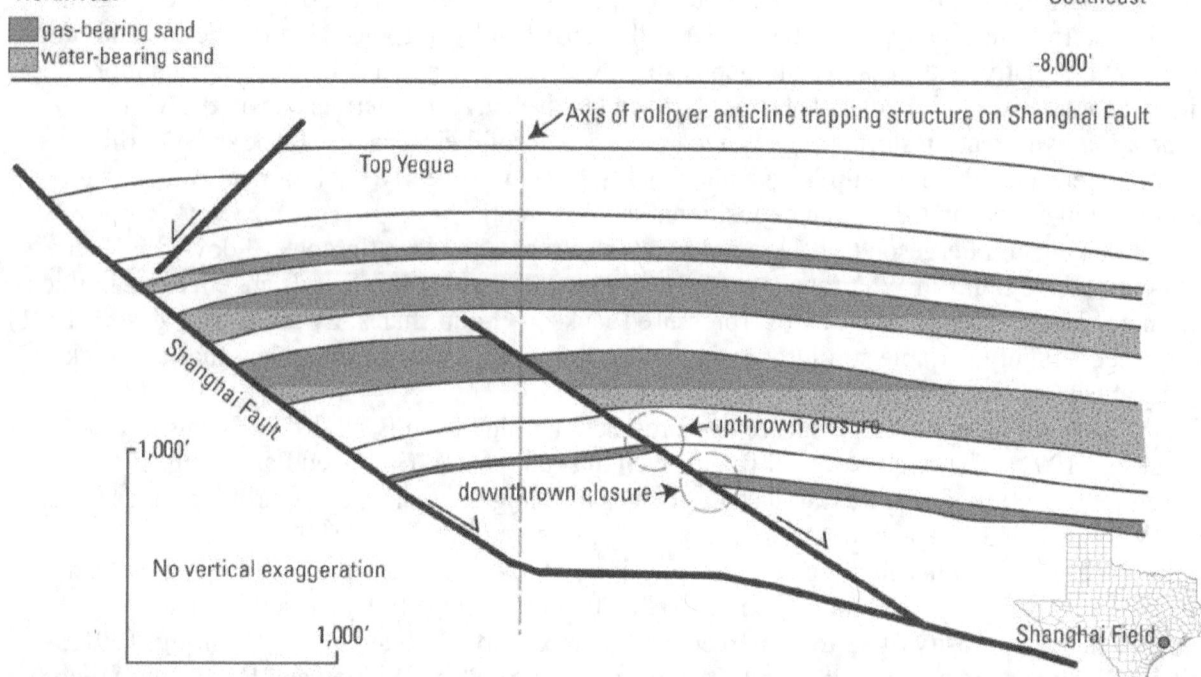

Figure 24. Cross section through Shanghai Field, Wharton County, Texas, in the expanded downdip Yegua trend (from Ewing and Fergeson, 1991). Shown are the different structural trapping styles common in Claiborne expanded fault zone reservoirs.

In areas impacted by salt tectonics, including the Houston Embayment and the Louisiana Salt Basins, traps against salt and (or) against faults created by salt movement are common. Broad stratal upwarping over deep-seated salt also is an important hydrocarbon trapping mechanism and is responsible for the two largest Claiborne discoveries, the Katy and the Conroe fields (fig. 6) of the Houston Embayment (described below). Salt movement is ongoing at present (Peel, 2007), suggesting that Claiborne hydrocarbon traps could be created in the present day.

Shellman (1985) described hydrocarbon accumulation in the updip Reklaw trend as fault controlled, citing down-to-the-basin faulting contemporaneous with sediment deposition. Shellman (1985) also described en echelon compensating antithetic up-to-the-coast faults, which are smaller than the major growth faults. In at least one case in Fayette County (fig. 6), up-to-the-coast faulting has created seals for the transgressive Reklaw sandstones by juxtaposing reservoirs with shale barriers (Shellman, 1985). Traps in the south Texas Yegua trend are both stratigraphic and structural, ranging from sand pinchouts to growth faults, due to the strandplain-barrier bar system depositional environment (West, 1963; Nehring, 1991).

Little has been reported regarding the quality of seals for Claiborne hydrocarbon accumulations. It typically is assumed that the permeability barrier created by sand-shale juxtaposition is sufficient to retard fluid movement. Nehring (1991) and Schenk and Viger (1996a) simply described seals for the lower, middle, and upper Claiborne units as shales of the same units. In addition, Nehring (1991) listed shales of the Jackson Group as seals for upper Claiborne Yegua reservoirs.

Influence of the Louann Salt

Evacuation and allochthonous flow of the Jurassic Louann Salt due to sedimentary loading have had a dramatic influence on the petroleum geology of the Gulf of Mexico Basin (McBride, 1998; McBride and others, 1998; Stover and others, 2001). In particular, the growth and emplacement of salt diapirs lead to the creation of complex structures which serve as petroleum migration pathways and traps (Halbouty, 1979). Stratigraphic units around salt dome margins are faulted by salt intrusion, creating fault traps, and are dragged upwards at the salt-rock contact, creating stratigraphic traps. Salt domes also may have mushroom-shaped caps, creating traps under overhanging edges (Schenk and Viger, 1996a). Upward migration of salt diapirs, which detach from the underlying autochthonous "mother salt," leaves behind complexly faulted stratal collapse zones which may also facilitate migration (Hood and others, 2002).

Salt evacuation and the creation of trapping features in concert with petroleum generation in the Gulf of Mexico potentially have been creating hydrocarbon accumulations since the Late Cretaceous (McBride, 1998; Stover and others, 2001), and possibly since shortly after the Callovian deposition of the Louann (Ewing, 1991). In the East Texas Basin, salt movement was initiated during the Late Jurassic, with diapirs forming during the Early Cretaceous (Ewing, 1991). Likewise, salt movement in the North Louisiana Salt Basin was initiated in the Late Jurassic through Cretaceous (Ewing, 1991). One-dimensional burial modeling by Lewan (2002) predicted Smackover oil generation as far back as 144 Ma adjacent to the Mississippi Salt Basin; this Upper Jurassic oil could have been trapped in structures created by salt movement. Elsewhere in the Gulf of Mexico, burial history models of Nelson and others (2000) predicted salt extrusion during the Eocene in south Louisiana, followed by evacuation through the Miocene. In the offshore area of Louisiana, salt extrusion did not occur until the Miocene (14.5 Ma) (Nelson and others, 2000). Maximum salt growth occurred following shelf margin progradation (Ewing, 1983).

Salt piercement diapirs have affected all of the Claiborne Group strata occurring in the Houston Embayment and Louisiana Salt Basins. According to Ewing (1991), shallow salt diapirs in the South Louisiana Salt Basin are small and cylindrical. In the Houston Embayment, salt diapirs reach near the surface, with tops generally less than 2,000 ft deep (Halbouty, 1979; Ewing, 1991). Diapirs frequently are aligned along major growth-fault trends, suggesting that preexisting domes influenced the initiation of faults and tended to control their location (Winker, 1982). Salt movement history is a critical component of understanding Claiborne hydrocarbon systems, particularly in the upper Claiborne Yegua of the Houston Embayment, where salt withdrawal may have influenced sand distribution and (or) trap integrity (Ewing, 2008).

Overview of Claiborne Exploration and Production History

The first production of a commercial Claiborne oil accumulation in Texas occurred in 1866 when L.T. Barrett brought in the No. 1 Isaac C. Skillern in Nacogdoches County (fig. 6), near the town of Oil Springs (Handbook of Texas Online, 2001). The discovery well flowed oil, water, and gas from a depth of 106 ft from a lower Claiborne sand and marked the discovery of the Nacogdoches field, the first Texas oil field. The Nacogdoches field still is marginally productive today, with stripper wells pumping oil from depths of 100 to 600 ft on seven active leases in 2004 (NRG Associates, 2006).

Oil discoveries made by searching for bubbling gas springs located over the region's numerous salt domes resulted in the 1901 discovery of the Spindletop and Jennings fields, in east Texas and southwestern Louisiana, respectively, and ushered in the great Gulf Coast oil boom of the early 1900s. More advanced exploration strategies led eventually to the discovery of giant Claiborne-reservoired oil fields over salt structures, including the oil- and gas-prone Conroe field 35 mi north of Houston in 1931 (fig. 25), and the nearby gas-condensate Katy field (fig. 6) in 1935 (Nehring, 1991). These early Claiborne discoveries primarily were made with geophysical prospecting techniques such as the torsion balance and with refraction and reflection seismograph surveys (Macelwane, 1940; Weatherby, 1940). The Conroe field grew quickly to over 19,000 acres and produced 65,000 barrels of oil per day (BO/day) in 1932, the third largest U.S. oil field at the time (American Oil and Gas Historical Society, 2005). Production primarily was from an upper Claiborne Cockfield Formation sand of 60 ft average thickness at approximately 5,050 ft average depth (Michaux and Buck, 1936). Conroe produced less than 2,000 BO/day in 2003; cumulative production through 2003 totaled about 730 million BO (NRG Associates, 2006). Development of the gas-condensate resources contained in the Katy field were slowed for a decade by the lack of a market for gas, and even 10 years after discovery, 85 percent of the daily allowable 450 million cubic feet of gas (MMCFG) production was being reinjected into the upper Claiborne reservoirs (Allison and others, 1946). Production was from six different Yegua and Cockfield sand zones at depths of 6,250 to 7,450 ft spread across a productive area of approximately 30,000 acres (Allison and others, 1946). Cumulative gas production at Katy through 2004 totaled around 5.9 trillion cubic feet of gas (TCFG) (however, see Kosters and others, 1989) with proved reserves of about 13.4 billion cubic feet of gas (BCFG) still in the ground (NRG Associates, 2006).

Upper Claiborne discoveries have continued mostly uninterrupted since the 1930s, with the development of 8,000- to 12,000-ft- deep downdip gas-condensate objectives beginning in the early 1980s (Nehring, 1991; Ewing and Fergeson, 1991; Ewing, 2008). In particular, the advent of three-dimensional (3-D) and amplitude versus offset (AVO) seismic techniques improved exploration success in the complicated lowstand depositional environment where small (<200 acres), isolated reservoir sands are highly compartmentalized by syndepositional growth faults and intervening shaley strata (Ewing and Fergeson, 1991; Ewing and Vincent, 1997b; McCuen and West, 1998; Ewing, 2001, 2008).

Exploration and discoveries in the lower Claiborne Queen City and Reklaw trends of south Texas spanned the decades of the 1950s through the 1980s (Nehring, 1991), with the discovery of deeper, downdip gas-condensate objectives in the 9,000- to 10,000-ft depth range occurring in the 1990s through the 2000s (NRG Associates, 2006). Application of 3-D seismic and AVO techniques also has contributed to better characterization of the non-associated gas accumulations in the deep, downdip objectives of the lower Claiborne, including Queen City reservoirs across the Rio Grande into the Burgos Basin of northern Mexico (Burnett, 1990; Tellez and others, 2002).

Resource Assessment

Based on source rock-reservoir rock elements of the petroleum system, the distribution of known fields and wells (IHS Energy Group 2005a, b; NRG Associates, 2006), and a geologic model describing the Cenozoic Gulf of Mexico depositional style, the Middle Eocene Claiborne Group was divided into seven conventional gas and oil assessment units. The lower Claiborne section includes four assessment units: Lower Claiborne Stable Shelf Gas and Oil (50470120), Lower Claiborne Expanded Fault Zone Gas (50470121), the hypothetical Lower Claiborne Slope and Basin Floor Gas (50470122), and the hypothetical Lower Claiborne Cane River (50470123). The upper Claiborne section includes three assessment units: Upper Claiborne Stable Shelf Gas and Oil (50470124), Upper Claiborne Expanded Fault Zone Gas (50470125), and the hypothetical Upper Claiborne Slope and Basin Floor Gas (50470126). The numbers in parentheses assigned for

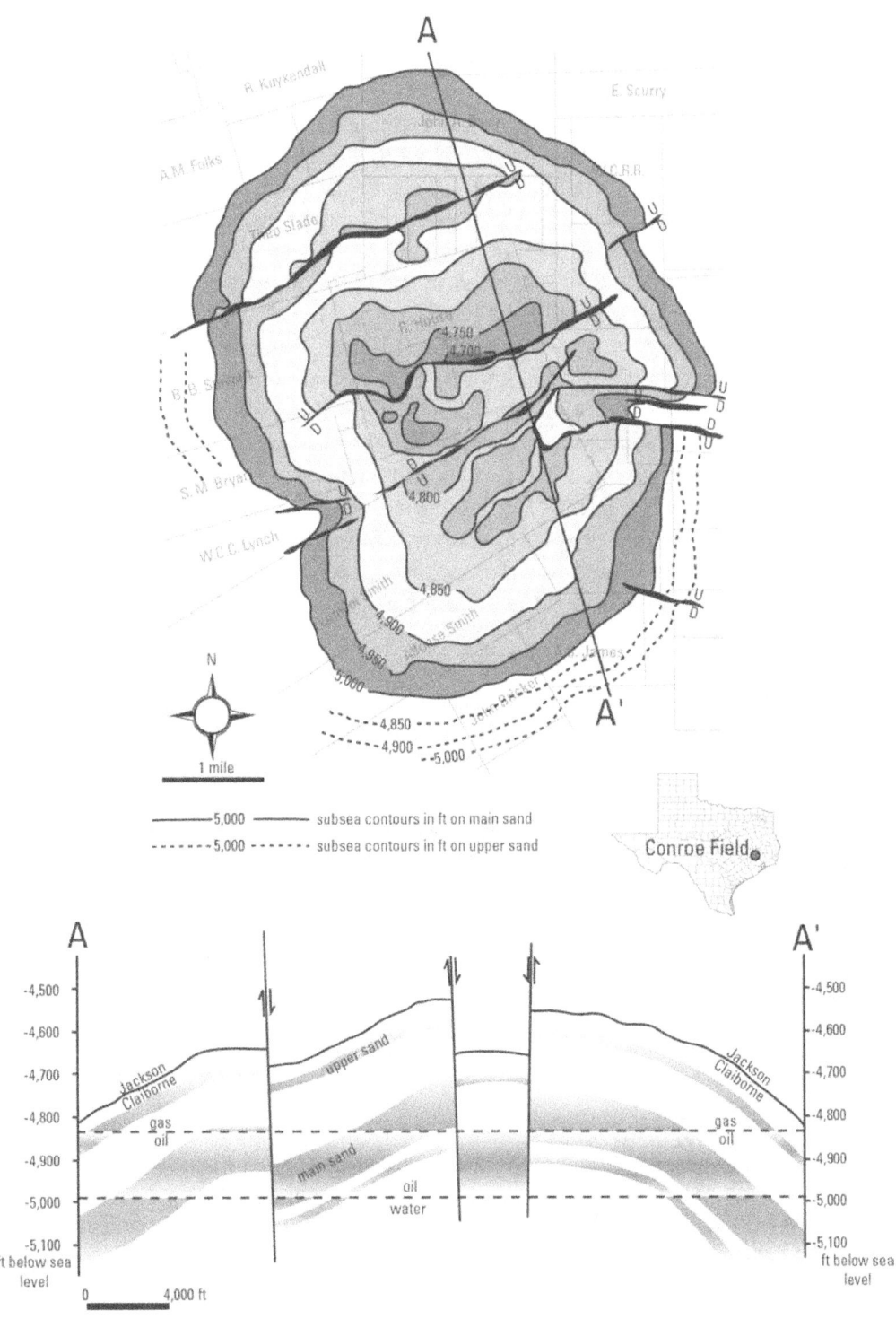

Figure 25. Map and diagrammatic cross section of the Conroe Field, Montgomery County, Texas (from Michaux and Buck, 1936). Lease names are shown in the plan view. Vertical exaggeration on cross section is approximately 20x. U = upthrown, D = downthrown.

each AU are a unique internal numerical identifier used in the USGS oil and gas assessment project. Summaries of the assessment unit characteristics and the input data used for resource assessment are tabulated in appendices A-G.

The geologic rationale for the seven Claiborne units used in this assessment can be summarized as follows. The Claiborne Group is stratigraphically divided into lower, middle, and upper sandstone reservoir facies (Queen City, Sparta, and Yegua/Cockfield) by regional transgressive marine facies rocks (Weches, Cook Mountain), creating three natural stratigraphic divisions (fig. 4A). For simplicity and because the lower Claiborne Queen City Sand is not present in the eastern part of the basin, the middle Claiborne Sparta and Cook Mountain strata were lumped with the upper Claiborne Yegua/Cockfield to create a twofold stratigraphic division: lower Claiborne Queen City and Reklaw reservoirs versus upper Claiborne Sparta, Yegua, Cook Mountain, and Cockfield reservoirs. Further justifying this division is the fact that Cook Mountain and Yegua reservoirs are inseparable in the NRG Associates (2006) database, from the point of analysis. In addition to the twofold stratigraphic division of Claiborne AUs, each of the upper and lower Claiborne was further divided into depositional facies of stable shelf, expanded fault zone, and slope and basin floor AUs (described in the "Geologic Model" section below). This resulted in the creation of six AUs to characterize the petroleum geology of the Claiborne. A seventh and final Claiborne AU, the hypothetical Lower Claiborne Cane River AU, was necessary so as to include the marine shelf facies of the lower Claiborne in the eastern part of the basin, from which there is no current or historical hydrocarbon production.

To complete the discovery history analysis that guided the estimation of undiscovered field numbers and sizes as presented herein, the assessment team first defined the geographic boundaries of the seven Claiborne AUs. The geologic rationale for the placement of the geographic boundaries of each AU is presented below. To assign reservoirs from the NRG Associates (2006) database to each AU, polygons representing the AU boundary were used in a GIS to clip Claiborne reservoirs. This step resulted in a spatial assignment of Claiborne reservoirs to the seven different AUs. In a final step, reservoirs were divided stratigraphically between the upper and lower Claiborne, so that each AU contained a determined 3-D volume of strata containing a certain number of Claiborne reservoirs. The characteristics (number of reservoirs, discovery year, size, gas-oil ratio, and so on) of those reservoirs as described in the NRG Associates (2006) database then were used to guide discovery history analysis for each AU, resulting in estimated numbers and sizes of undiscovered fields as per the methodology described in Klett and others (2003). Estimated numbers and sizes of undiscovered fields were used in a Monte Carlo simulation to calculate mean and fractile undiscovered resource volumes (Charpentier and Klett, 2005).

Comparisons with the 1995 Assessment

The 1995 oil and gas assessment of the Gulf Coast Basin (Schenk and Viger, 1996a, b) included four plays composed exclusively of Claiborne strata: 4724, Middle Eocene Sandstones Downdip Gas (Queen City and Cook Mountain reservoirs); 4725, Middle Eocene Sandstones Updip Fluvial Oil and Gas (Queen City, Reklaw, and Sparta reservoirs); 4726, Yegua Updip Fluvial-Deltaic Oil and Gas (Yegua and Cockfield reservoirs); and 4727, Yegua Downdip Gas (Yegua and Cockfield reservoirs). The 1995 assessment also included some Claiborne reservoirs with strata of other ages in two additional plays: 4701, Houston Salt Dome Flank Oil and Gas; and 4945, Wilcox Salt Basins Oil. In contrast, this assessment places known Queen City and Reklaw reservoirs into the two updip Lower Claiborne AUs (50470120, 50470121), and all other known Claiborne reservoirs (Cook Mountain, Sparta, Yegua, and Cockfield) are placed into the two updip

Upper Claiborne AUs (50470124, 50470125). The 3-D volumes of rock placed into the three hypothetical Claiborne AUs of this assessment (50470122, 50470123, 50470126) were not considered in the 1995 assessment. Reservoirs that were included in the 4701 Houston Salt Dome Flank Oil and Gas and the 4945 Wilcox Salt Basins Oil plays of the 1995 assessment are included in the Upper Claiborne Stable Shelf Gas and Oil AU (50470124) of this assessment.

Geologic Model

Assessment of undiscovered resources in the Paleogene Gulf of Mexico Basin was based on a geologic model that describes the progradation of structural and depositional systems of reservoir rocks in "stable shelf," "expanded fault zone," and "slope and basin floor" environments (fig. 26A). This model is developed from the detailed analyses of Cenozoic depositional systems in the Gulf Basin that illustrated recurring depositional and structural themes for all of the clastic stratigraphy (Winker, 1982; Galloway, 1989; Galloway and others, 2000; Galloway, 2005). In particular, each Paleogene clastic package illustrates either a period of dominant progradation into the Gulf of Mexico (Wilcox, Vicksburg, Frio) or progradation interrupted by periods of regional highstand and deposition of transgressive shale (Claiborne, Jackson). During dominantly progradational periods, deposition occurred in stable shelf environments on the landward margin of the basin, in expanded fault zone environments at the contemporary shelf edge, and in slope and basin floor environments basinward of the contemporary shelf edge. This motif is repeated in each of the progradational clastic packages, resulting in a stepping-out effect of the three environments into the Gulf of Mexico during deposition of each overlying stratigraphic package.

Within individual stratigraphic packages (for example, the Wilcox or Claiborne Groups), the boundaries between the structural-depositional environments are time transgressive (fig. 26B). For example, during progradation of clastic packages into the Gulf of Mexico, the shelf margin gradually advances basinward, in effect bringing stable shelf structural-depositional environments over the previously deposited expansion zone within the same stratigraphic package (the Wilcox or Claiborne Group). In other words, the real boundaries between the structural-depositional environments overlap in plan view and overlap in the depth range of reservoirs. For the purposes of the assessment and for the analysis of exploration and production history of individual AUs, this overlap has the unintended consequence of misplacing discovered reservoirs which lie near the structural-depositional boundary between the stable shelf and expanded fault zone environments. Thus, characteristics of two AUs may be unintentionally lumped at their margins into one dataset. Some evidence of this overlap is present in the analysis of 50470124, the Upper Claiborne Stable Shelf Gas and Oil AU. In figure 27, gas accumulation sizes for 50470124 are plotted as a function of discovery year. Following development of the expanded downdip Yegua trend in the early 1980s, a jump in accumulation sizes from the established downward-tailing trend of the stable shelf environment is recorded as a result of the time-transgressive overlap of the two depositional environments at their margins.

Stable Shelf

Each of the three conceptualized environments of the geologic model contains a distinct set of predictable features. In the landward stable shelf environment, relatively shallow (mostly <8,000 ft in Claiborne) reservoirs are characterized by minimal expansion due to growth faulting and primarily consist of highstand and transgressive systems tracts, including regional fluvial-deltaic complexes, delta mouth and barrier bars, shelf sandstones, and incised valley fill (fig. 28). Reservoir facies have high and predictable lateral continuity. Traps generally are against

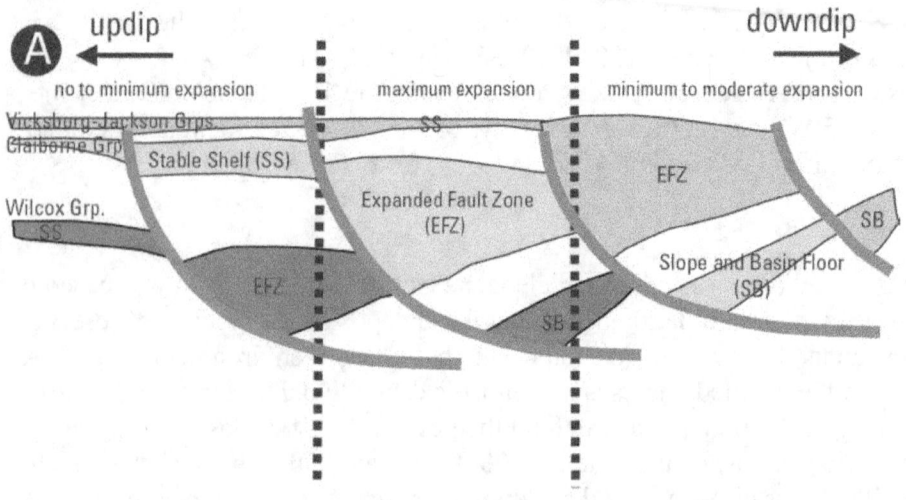

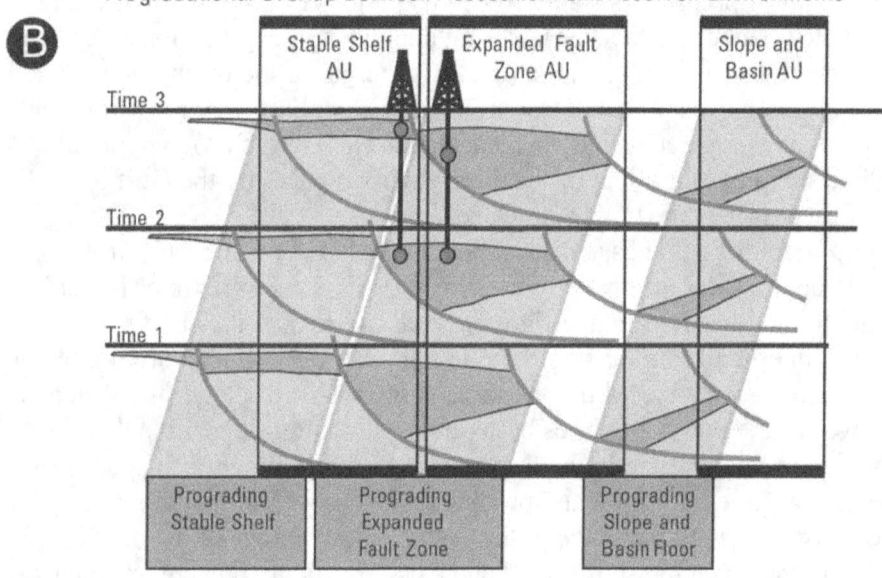

Figure 26. Conceptualized geologic model used for this assessment. A, Two-dimensional geologic model illustrating sequence of stable shelf, expanded fault zone, and slope and basin floor environments (from Warwick and others, 2007). The beige polygons labeled "Stable Shelf (SS)," "Expanded Fault Zone (EFZ)," and "Slope and Basin Floor (SB)" represent the environments of the Claiborne Group and correspond to the descriptors "no to minimum expansion," "maximum expansion," and "minimum to moderate expansion," respectively. The green polygons represent the environments of the overlying Jackson Group and Vicksburg Formation, and the blue polygons represent the environments of the underlying Wilcox Group. B, Time-transgressive nature of geologic model environments showing the overlap of environments and therefore the overlap of assessment unit (AU) characteristics at their boundaries.

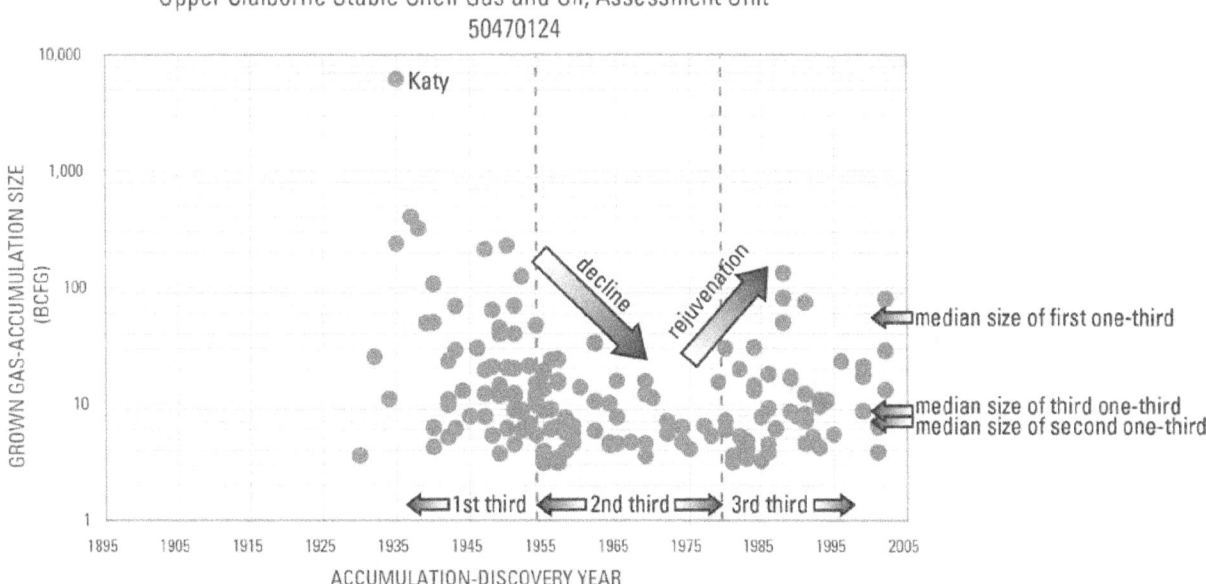

Figure 27. Gas accumulation sizes for the Upper Claiborne Stable Shelf Gas and Oil Assessment Unit (AU) (50470124) plotted as a function of discovery year. Accumulations are divided into thirds by year of discovery. Note that the median size of the third one-third of discovered reservoirs is larger than the median size of the second one-third. The growth in sizes of discovered reservoirs beginning in the early 1980s is a result of inclusion in this AU of reservoirs discovered as part of the development of the middip-downdip Yegua expanded fault zone trend (Ewing, 2008). The regional-scale nature of this assessment precludes precise division of the AUs at their boundaries, resulting in AUs which contain characteristics of more than one environment. Data are from NRG Associates (2006), plotted by T. Klett, USGS. BCFG, billion cubic feet of gas.

reactivated growth faults which sole out in the underlying strata. Less frequent are back-barrier pinchout stratigraphic traps (except in south Texas Claiborne back-barrier facies environments). Reservoirs are normally pressured, usually produce both oil and associated gas, and typically have a high water cut. This is a mature Claiborne exploration and production trend, with few remaining undiscovered fields and little potential for field growth via infill.

Expanded Fault Zone

The expanded fault zone environment occurs over a relatively narrow area in plan view, bracketing the contemporary Claiborne shelf edge basinward of the stable shelf. Reservoirs are characterized by maximum stratigraphic expansion over syndepositional growth faults. Cumulative reservoir thickness is large; individual sands typically are thicker, although not always, than those in the stable shelf environment. Reservoir sandstones consist of deep (mostly 8,000–14,000 ft) highstand and lowstand systems tracts including delta mouth and delta front facies, incised valley fill, outer shelf storm retreat sands, and upper slope sands occurring in turbidite deposits and slump blocks (fig. 28). Reservoir facies have low and hard-to-predict lateral continuity. Traps are associated with the ubiquitous contemporary growth faults, including rollover anticlines and upthrown and downthrown fault closures. Reservoirs are overpressured and flow chiefly non-associated gas and condensate. A few oil fields also are present. Fields are highly

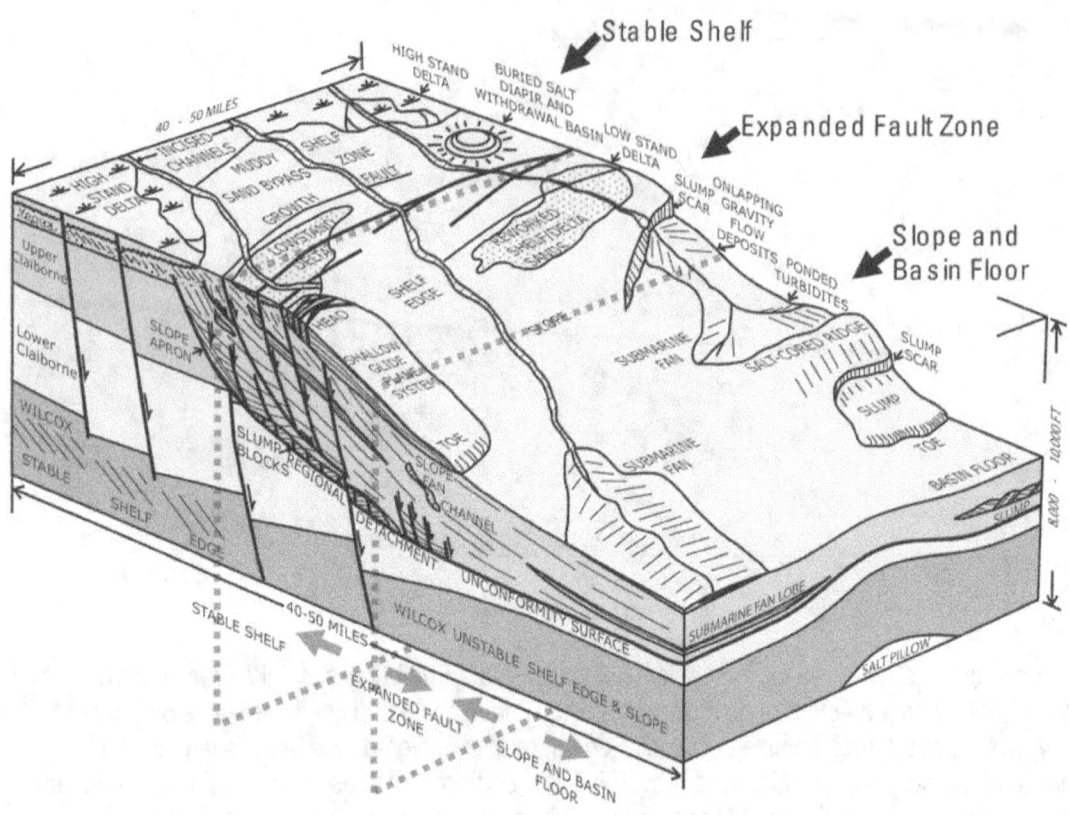

Figure 28. Schematic block diagram illustrating location and type of depositional environments and assessment unit elements of the geologic model (from Edwards, 1991).

compartmentalized and smaller in areal extent compared to the stable shelf. For the Claiborne, this is a late frontier to mature exploration and production trend with a high likelihood for new discoveries and excellent potential for existing field infill.

Slope and Basin Floor

The slope and basin floor environment occurs downdip of the expanded fault zone and is characterized by minimal expansion of Claiborne reservoir sands due to the distal nature of deposition from contemporaneous shelf edge growth faulting. Deep reservoir sandstones (mostly >12,000 ft) consist of lowstand systems tracts including slope turbidite fans and channels, slope apron fans, shelf slump sands, incised valley fill, and blanket sand deposits on the basin floor (fig. 28). Reservoir facies can be laterally continuous, but their locations are a challenge to predict or project from shallower, overlying strata or from updip environments. Traps include stratigraphic pinchouts at sand body margins, complicated by structural offset resulting from growth faults which sole out from the overlying expansion zone. Reservoirs are overpressured, high-temperature, and flow non-associated gas and condensate. Reservoir quality is a risk factor, due to porosity-permeability loss from increasing burial depth (Dutton and Loucks, 2008). Recent Paleogene discoveries in the distal offshore Gulf of Mexico indicate that the deep basinal Claiborne Group contains very little sand in the present-day deepwater environment (Meyer and others, 2005). However, the data presented by Meyer and others (2005) are for a well almost 200 mi offshore

Texas; the shelf margin bypass predicted by Swenson (1997) would deliver sands directly into Claiborne slope and basin floor environments.

In the Claiborne, the slope and basin floor environment is a hypothetical exploration and production trend with very high potential for new discoveries. To date, high per-well costs, coupled with the fact that the major operators currently are investing primarily in offshore exploration, have significantly limited development in this frontier area.

Data Supporting the Geologic Model

Aspects of the geologic model described above were drawn from the voluminous literature describing Cenozoic patterns of sediment deposition in the Gulf Basin (Winker, 1982; Ewing and Fergeson, 1991; Edwards, 1991; Galloway and others, 2000; Galloway, 2005). For this assessment, an analysis of the petroleum geology data contained in the NRG Associates (2006) database was performed to see if the data contained therein support the geologic model. To make the analysis, Claiborne reservoir data in the NRG Associates (2006) database were first divided into upper and lower Claiborne stratigraphic units (previously described) and then separated by depth-to-reservoir into those >8,000 ft and <8,000 ft deep. Eight thousand feet was chosen as a regional approximation of the break between stable shelf and onset of the expanded fault zone. This is somewhat simplified; in south Texas the onset of the expanded zone is closer to 7,500 ft, whereas in south Louisiana the expanded zone is deeply buried under the Oligocene-Miocene and is closer to 9,000 to 10,000 ft. However, 8,000 ft was selected as the most appropriate depth in the regional approach taken herein.

As depicted in figure 29, Claiborne reservoirs >8,000 ft deep spatially occur at the basinward margin of discovered Claiborne hydrocarbon accumulations and bracket the contemporary shelf margins of Galloway and others (2000). As described above, some reservoirs >8,000 ft deep occur in the stable shelf environment in southern Louisiana, where the expanded fault zone is more deeply buried, and some reservoirs <8,000 ft deep occur in the expanded zone in south Texas (fig. 29). Data from the NRG Associates (2006) database indicate that the deeper, more basinward reservoirs are at higher average temperature and pressure and have lower average porosity and permeability. In general, reservoirs >8,000 ft deep are overpressured (fig. 30). This is perhaps the best indicator of occurrence in the expansion zone; industry experience indicates that *all* discovered expanded fault zone reservoirs in the Claiborne are overpressured (T.E. Ewing, Frontera Exploration Consultants, Inc., written commun., 2008). NRG Associates (2006) data also indicate that basinward reservoirs produce lighter petroleum products than landward reservoirs (median 51° API gravity versus 44° API gravity). Finally, basinward reservoirs, which are interpreted to have been deposited in the zone of maximum expansion, have a greater average reservoir thickness (57 ft; n = 183) than the landward reservoirs (33 ft; n = 510), which are interpreted to have been deposited on the contemporary shelf. Although relatively simplistic, this basic analysis confirms the first-order prediction of the geologic model, namely, reservoir expansion at the contemporary shelf edge.

Lower Claiborne Stable Shelf Gas and Oil (50470120)

The Lower Claiborne Stable Shelf Gas and Oil AU lies entirely within Texas, extending northeast from the international border to within about 20 mi of the Louisiana border, encompassing an area of about 25.4 million acres (fig. 31). The AU boundaries were defined on the north, northwest, and west by the outcrop limit in Texas. These boundaries were placed slightly basinward of the limit of Claiborne outcrop to account for the presence of very shallow historical

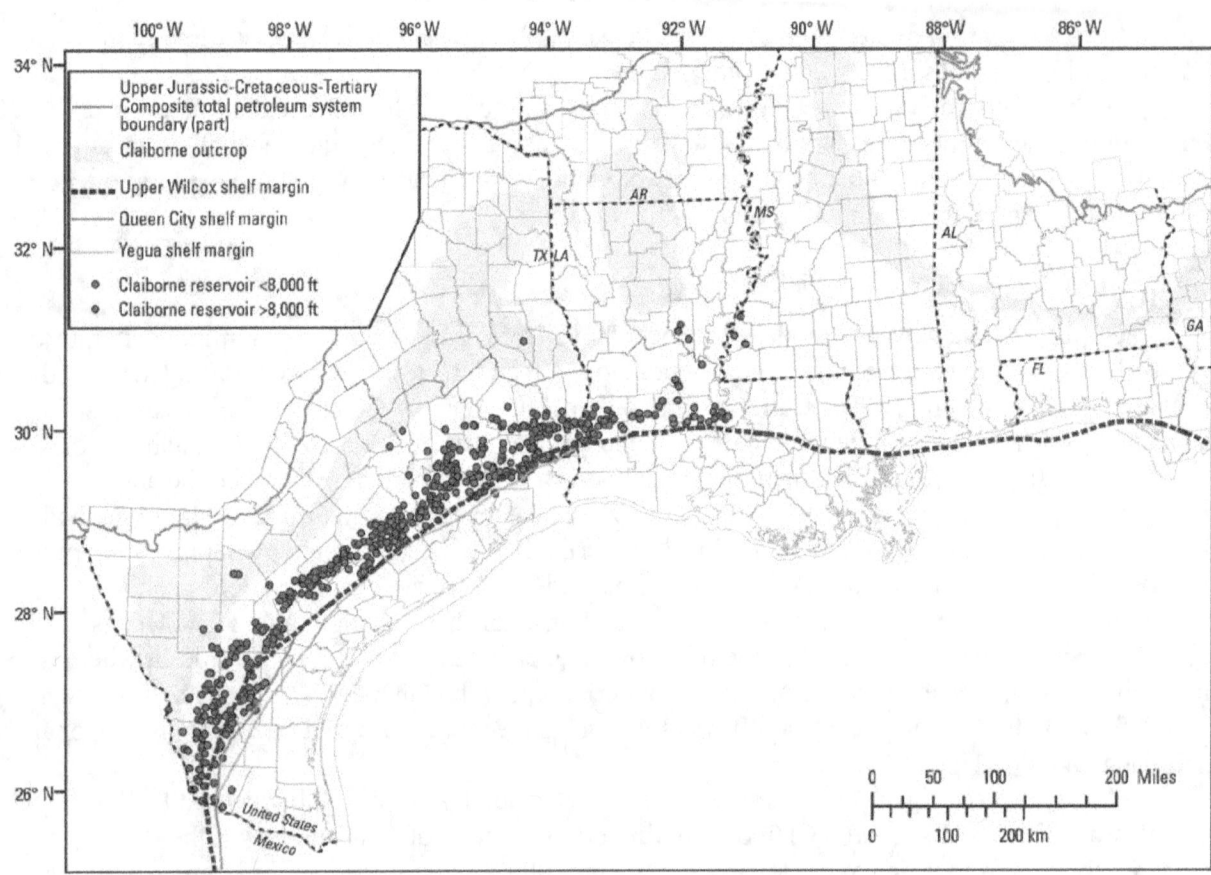

Figure 29. Spatial distribution of Claiborne reservoirs that are <8,000 feet depth-to-top and >8,000 feet depth-to-top. Claiborne Group outcrop is from Schruben and others (1994); upper Wilcox and Claiborne (Queen City and Yegua) shelf margins are from Galloway and others (2000); location of Claiborne reservoirs is from NRG Associates (2006).

and current oil production. Sand input to the basin was limited to the Rio Grande Embayment during this time and, therefore, the eastern AU boundary was placed near the Texas-Louisiana boundary. On the southwest, the AU boundary was drawn at the international border. To the southeast, the AU boundary corresponds to the underlying upper Wilcox shelf margin, which matches the updip limit of the adjacent Lower Claiborne Expanded Fault Zone AU (50470121). Noncommercial to minor production is located in the area of the Queen City sand maxima, probably due to lack of thick shale seals and thinning of potential source beds (Guevara and García, 1972). Hydrocarbon products predominantly are gas and medium to light oil.

The Lower Claiborne Stable Shelf Gas and Oil AU is an established exploration and production trend with 16 oil and 39 gas accumulations that exceed the minimum size considered in this assessment (0.5 MMBO and 3 BCFG for oil and gas accumulations, respectively). The median grown size of discovered gas accumulations, when divided into thirds (by early, middle, and late initial dates of discovery) is 13.4, 7.7, and 5.2 BCFG (fig. 32A), indicating moderate and consistent decline with time, and for discovered oil accumulations is 1.5, 2.8, and 1.6 MMBO (fig. 32B). The increase in grown sizes between the first and second thirds of discovered oil accumulations may reflect early discovery of shallow, smaller accumulations drilled on obvious structures

44

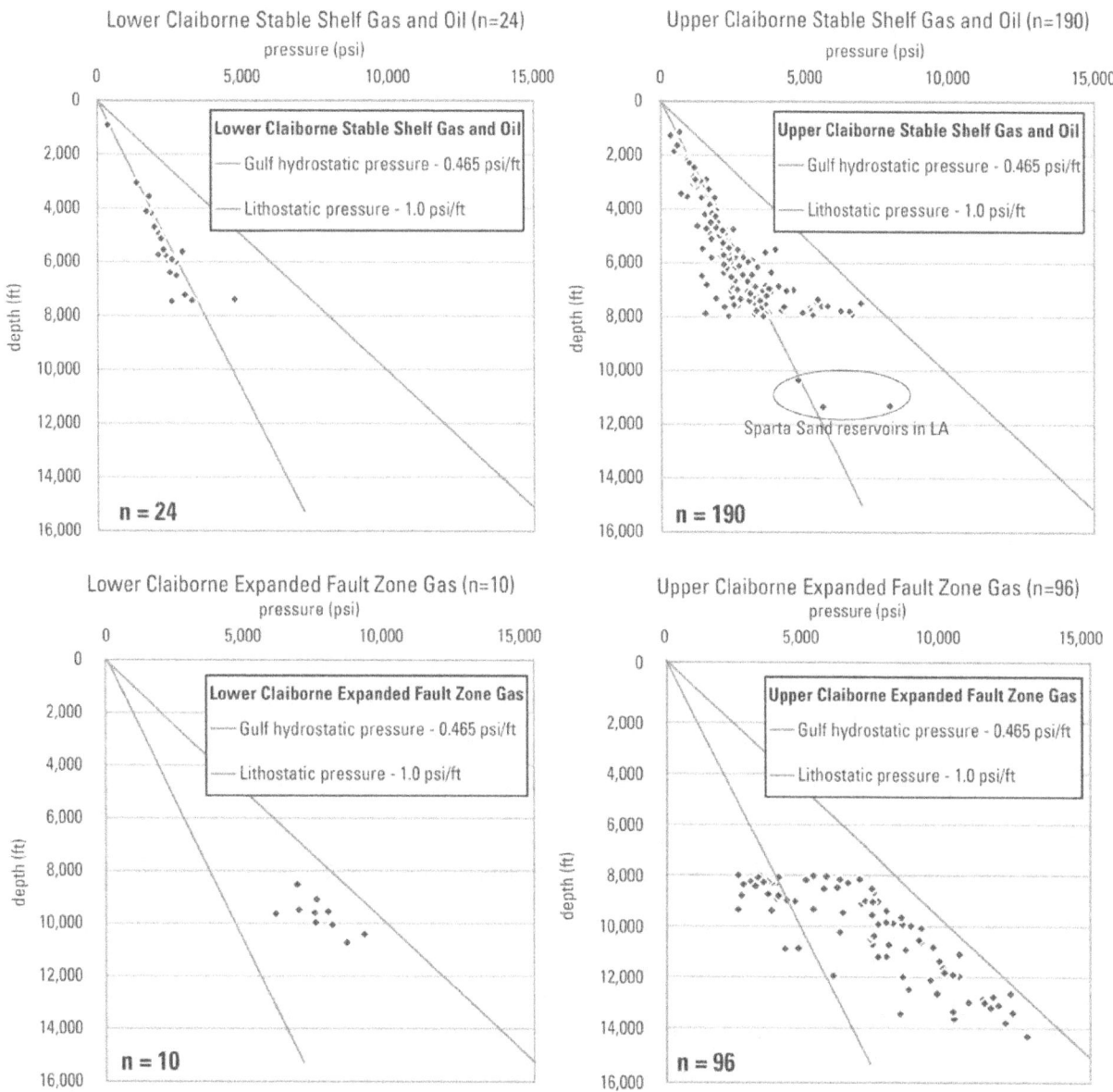

Figure 30. Plots of pressure as a function of depth for Claiborne reservoirs with pressure data (data from NRG Associates, 2006, including initial reservoir, initial shut-in well head, and initial shut-in bottom hole pressures). Data are divided into reservoirs that are <8,000 feet deep and >8,000 feet deep; 8,000 foot depth is a regional approximation to the onset of overpressure in the Claiborne Group and is only an approximate depth for the boundary between stable shelf and expanded fault zone reservoirs. The regional-scale nature of this assessment precludes precise division of the stable shelf and expanded fault zone reservoirs, resulting in the overlap of pressure characteristics shown here. Gulf hydrostatic pressure line is from Dickinson (1953). Deeply buried Sparta Sand reservoirs in Louisiana indicate mostly normally pressured stable shelf conditions. psi = pounds per square inch.

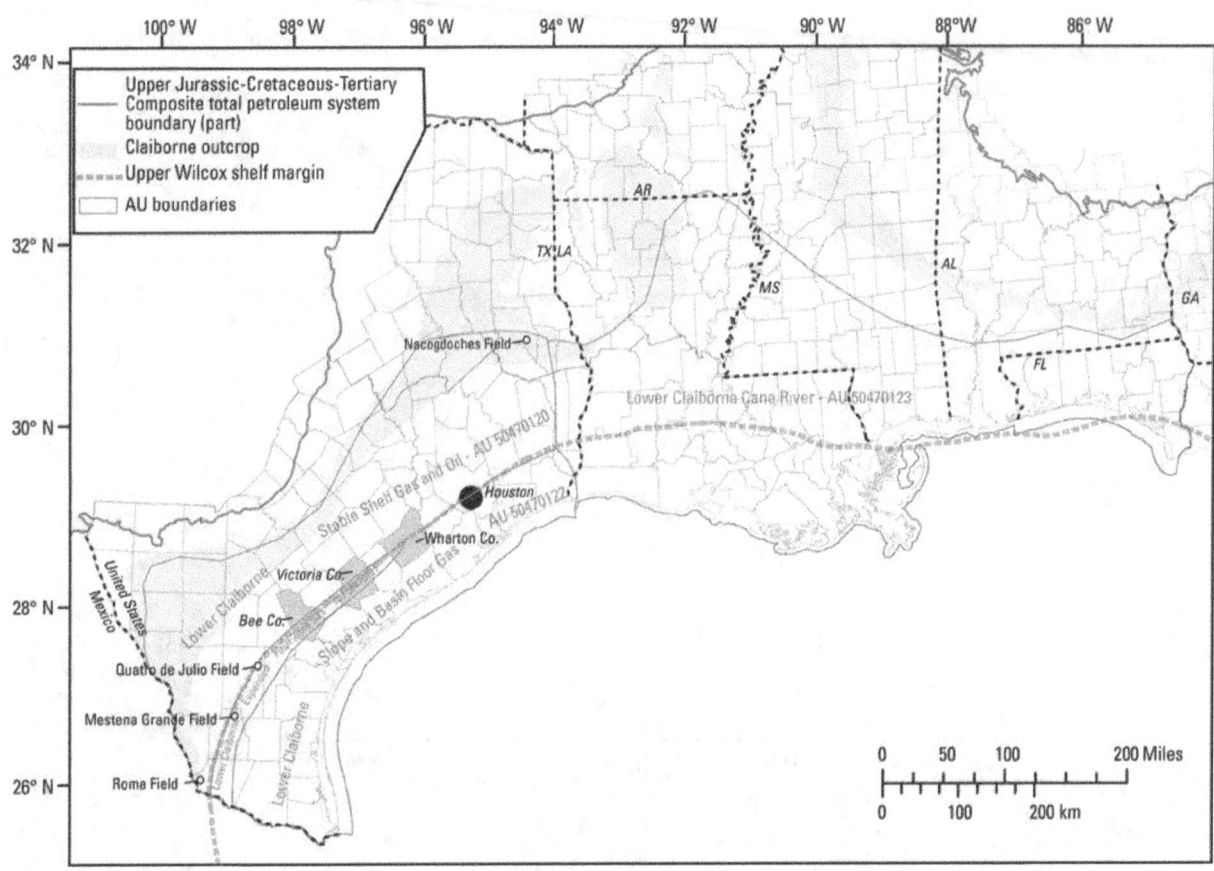

Figure 31. Map showing extent of lower Claiborne assessment units (AU). Claiborne Group outcrop is from Schruben and others (1994); Wilcox Group shelf margin is from Galloway and others (2000). Co. = County.

(e.g., Nacogdoches field, 1866; Roma field, 1929; figs. 31 and 32B), followed later (1950s) by larger discoveries at greater depths. "Grown" size indicates that a reserve growth function was applied to the known hydrocarbon volumes in discovered reservoirs (for an explanation of methodology see Attanasi and Root, 1994). Grown discovered oil accumulations total 40.5 MMBO and grown discovered gas accumulations total 831 BCFG for this AU. The AU was considered to contain one or more undiscovered hydrocarbon accumulations on the basis of having adequate charge, reservoir rocks, and favorable timing of geologic events (generation, migration, and accumulation of petroleum resources).

The number of undiscovered oil accumulations is estimated to be a minimum of one, a maximum of 15, and a mode of 5. At the maximum, 15 undiscovered oil accumulations were predicted; however, the mode of 5 undiscovered accumulations reflects that this area is maturely explored. Sizes of oil accumulations were estimated to be a minimum of 0.5 MMBO (minimum cutoff size considered in this assessment), a maximum of 3 MMBO, and a median of 1 MMBO. The maximum size of 3 MMBO was selected to allow for the possibility that an undiscovered field could equal approximately 40 percent of the grown size of the largest discovered oil accumulation. The median size of 1 MMBO was selected as consistent with the sizes of accumulations discovered over the last 40 years and considering decline between the median of the second and third thirds of

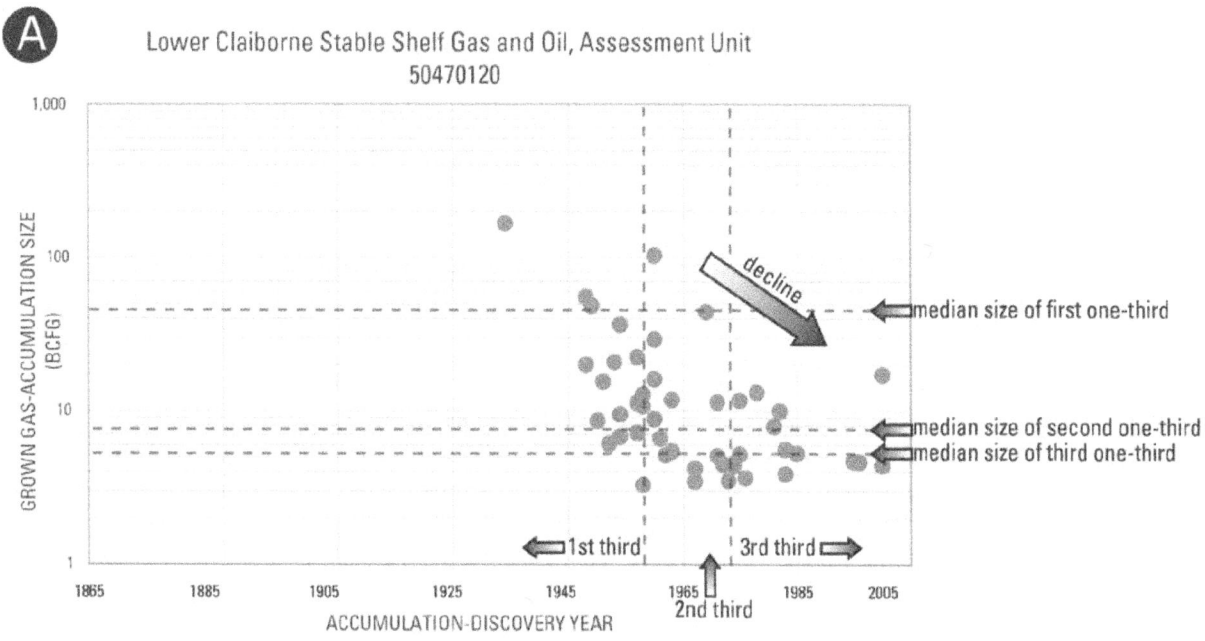

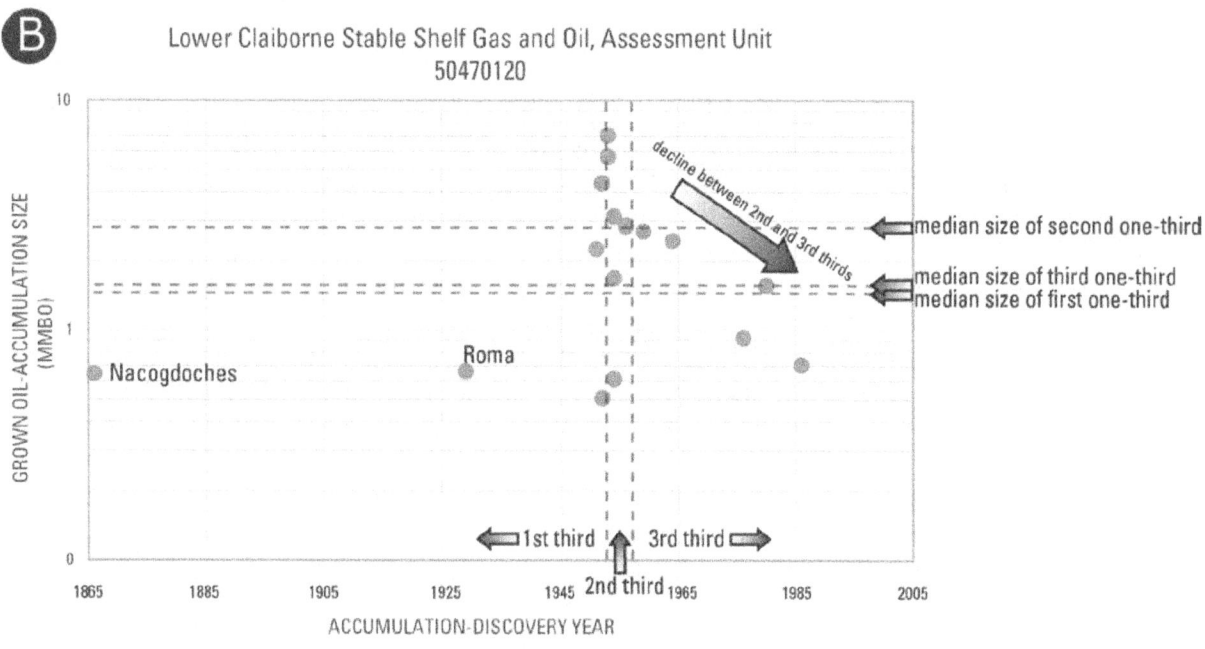

Figure 32. Gas and oil discovery curves for the Lower Claiborne Stable Shelf Gas and Oil assessment unit (AU). A, Grown gas accumulation sizes for the Lower Claiborne Stable Shelf Gas and Oil AU (50470120) plotted as a function of discovery year. B, Grown oil accumulation sizes for the Lower Claiborne Stable Shelf Gas and Oil AU (50470120) plotted as a function of discovery year. Data from NRG Associates (2006), plotted by T. Klett, USGS. BCFG = billion cubic feet of gas, MMBO = million barrels of oil.

discovered accumulations (2.8 and 1.6 MMBO, respectively, fig. 32B). Reservoir depths for oil accumulations are expected to range between 400 and 8,000 ft. .

Numbers of undiscovered gas accumulations were estimated to be a minimum of 1, a maximum of 30, and a mode of 10. The maximum number of 30 undiscovered gas accumulations was selected to account for the possibility of new discoveries at the least explored, deepest downdip basinward margin of the AU, near the boundary with the Lower Claiborne Fault Zone AU (50470121). The mode of 10 undiscovered accumulations was selected because a similar number of fields have been discovered in the AU in the last three decades, indicating good potential for future gas accumulation discoveries. Sizes of undiscovered gas accumulations were estimated to be a minimum of 3 BCFG (minimum cutoff size considered in this assessment), a maximum of 40 BCFG, and a median of 4 BCFG. The maximum size was selected to allow for the possibility that an undiscovered field could equal 25 percent of the largest discovered field. The median of 4 BCFG for undiscovered gas accumulations reflects a value consistent with the size of discoveries made in the last three decades and incorporating decline from the median size of the last third of discovered reservoirs (5.2 BCFG, fig. 32A). Reservoir depths for gas accumulations are expected to range between 900 and 8,000 ft.

Mean estimates of undiscovered resources for the Lower Claiborne Stable Shelf Gas and Oil AU from Monte Carlo simulation are 7 MMBO, 88 BCFG, and 2 million barrels of natural gas liquids (MMBNGL) (table 1). Table 1 also shows estimated hydrocarbon resources for the F95, F50, and F5 fractiles (F95 equals a 95 percent chance of at least the amount tabulated; other fractiles are defined similarly).

The most recently discovered hydrocarbon reservoir in the assessment unit was the Cuatro de Julio field (fig. 31) in 2000. This is one of the deepest and most basinward reservoirs in the assessment unit and one of seven gas discoveries in the last 20 years. The last oil discovery in the AU was in 1980. This AU also contains the Nacogdoches field (fig. 31), discovered in 1866 and the first oil field in Texas.

An estimated 19,970 new field wildcat wells penetrate the top of the Yegua in this AU, for an approximate high-side exploration density of 1 wildcat well for every 2.0 mi^2 (assuming the wells reach the lower Claiborne at total depth; see below for additional explanation). Moderate potential for undiscovered hydrocarbon reservoirs is expected to be found in deep gas accumulations occurring in structural traps located near the basinward margin of the AU, as well as some small oil accumulations in stratigraphic traps.

The number of new field wildcat wells reaching the top of the Claiborne for this AU and the other AUs described below was determined as follows. For each AU, the total depth of the new field wildcat wells coded in the IHS database was compared in a GIS with a structural top-of-Claiborne grid (fig. 13) constructed from stratigraphic tops information also contained in the IHS database. New field wildcats that did not penetrate the top of the Claiborne were discarded. At the downdip margin of the top-of-Claiborne grid, data quality is degraded by fewer penetrations; therefore, top-of-Vicksburg and top-of-Frio grids also were used (adding approximate Claiborne thicknesses) to estimate wildcat penetrations to the top of the Claiborne, particularly for the hypothetical Lower and Upper Claiborne Slope and Basin Floor AUs. This exercise overestimates the level of exploration because many of the wildcats do not penetrate the complete Claiborne section, but it is arguably the best approach available for the regional nature of this assessment.

A low-side approach to estimating the numbers of new field wildcat wells testing the entire Claiborne section would be to use top-of-Wilcox penetrations. However, in some of the Claiborne AUs, particularly in the downdip areas of the hypothetical AUs, the number of top-of-Wilcox

Table 1. Mean and fractile estimates of undiscovered resources in the Claiborne Group.

[MMBO = million barrels of oil, BCFG = billion cubic feet of gas, NGL = natural gas liquid, MMBNGL = million barrels of natural gas liquids]

Total Petroleum Systems (TPS) and Assessment Units (AU)	Field Type	Total Undiscovered Resources											
		Oil (MMBO)				Gas (BCFG)				NGL (MMBNGL)			
		F95	F50	F5	Mean	F95	F50	F5	Mean	F95	F50	F5	Mean
Upper Jurassic-Cretaceous-Tertiary Composite, TPS 504701													
Lower Claiborne Stable Shelf Gas and Oil, AU 50470120	Oil	3	7	13	7		19	40	21	0	0	1	0
	Gas					21	63	124	67	0	2	3	2
Lower Claiborne Expanded Fault Zone Gas, AU 50470121	Oil	1	3	8	4		16	43	19	0	1	3	1
	Gas					351	942	1,767	987	13	37	76	39
Lower Claiborne Slope and Basin Floor Gas, Au 50470122	Oil	0	0	0	0		0	0	0	0	0	0	0
	Gas					573	3,195	8,044	3,620	21	124	338	145
Lower Claiborne Cane River, AU 50470123	Oil	Not quantitatively assessed											
	Gas												
Upper Claiborne Stable Shelf Gas and Oil, AU 50470124	Oil	4	12	23	13	12	36	78	40	0	1	2	1
	Gas					97	357	858	402	3	10	25	11
Upper Claiborne Expanded Fault Zone Gas, AU 50470125	Oil	8	26	53	28	39	128	287	142	3	9	21	10
	Gas					1,417	4,386	9,096	4,740	95	307	698	341
Upper Claiborne Slope and Basin Floor Gas, AU 50470126	Oil	0	0	0	0	0	0	0	0	0	0	0	0
	Gas					1,706	8,147	19,632	9,107	116	569	1,489	655
Total		Total Mean Oil 52				Total Mean Gas 19,145				Total Mean NGL 1,205			

49

penetrations is very low or zero. Because of this fact, a poorly constructed top-of-Wilcox grid results; thus, comparing total depth of new field wildcats to the grid is dubious. Therefore, the high-side approach of using the top-of-Yegua grid was accepted as the best compromise in determining exploration density for this assessment.

Lower Claiborne Expanded Fault Zone Gas (50470121)

The Lower Claiborne Expanded Fault Zone Gas AU lies entirely within southern Texas, extending northeast from the international border to Wharton County, where it tapers out against the Lower Claiborne Stable Shelf Gas and Oil AU, about 65 mi southwest of Houston (fig. 31). The AU covers an area of about 2.3 million acres. The boundary on the northwest is defined by the southern boundary of the Lower Claiborne Stable Shelf Gas and Oil AU (50470120), corresponding to the updip limit of reservoir expansion over the underlying upper Wilcox shelf margin. The southwestern boundary was drawn at the international border. To the east, the AU boundary is limited by distance from sand input in the Rio Grande Embayment, and a more conservative eastern boundary than chosen herein may be considered in the area of Bee County (fig. 31) (T.E. Ewing, Frontera Exploration Consultants, Inc., written commun., 2008). On the southeast, the AU boundary is constituted by the theoretical downdip limit of expansion, representing the distal limit of the prograding lower Claiborne shelf margin and approximately corresponding to the updip limit of the overlying upper Claiborne expansion zone.

The Lower Claiborne Expanded Fault Zone Gas AU is a frontier exploration trend with 10 discovered gas accumulations that exceed the minimum size considered for this assessment (3 BCFG for gas accumulations). Grown discovered gas accumulations total 404 BCFG. The median grown size of discovered gas accumulations, when divided into halves (by early and later initial dates of production), is 9.7 and 35.1 BCFG, indicating an increase in the size of discovered gas accumulations with time (fig. 33A). There are no discovered oil accumulations in the AU greater than the minimum cutoff size (0.5 MMBO). The AU was considered to contain one or more undiscovered hydrocarbon accumulations on the basis of having adequate charge, reservoir rocks, and favorable timing of geologic events.

The number of undiscovered oil accumulations is estimated to be a minimum of one, a maximum of five, and a mode of two. The maximum of five and mode of two for undiscovered oil accumulations were selected to reflect the fact that this is an overall gas-prone AU, while not discounting the possibility that some small undiscovered oil accumulations may be present in subtle structural traps. Sizes of oil accumulations were estimated to be a minimum of 0.5 MMBO (minimum cutoff size), a maximum of 15 MMBO, and a median of 1 MMBO. The maximum number of 15 MMBO was selected because (1) the AU is under-explored and (2) the assessment team wanted to emphasize that sand delivery in the Rio Grande Embayment to lowstand systems tracts in the lower Claiborne may provide for substantial untested reservoir acreage in the downdip environment. The median value of 1 MMBO was selected to be consistent with and slightly lower than the median size (1.6 MMBO) of the most recently discovered fields in the updip Lower Claiborne AU (50470120). Reservoir depths for oil accumulations are expected to range between 8,000 and 14,000 ft.

Numbers of undiscovered gas accumulations were estimated to be a minimum of 5, a maximum of 50, and a mode of 25. The maximum of 50 was selected because this is a relatively under-explored frontier area with only three decades of activity. The mode of 25 was selected to reflect the consistent and steady nature of discoveries since the trend was opened in the early

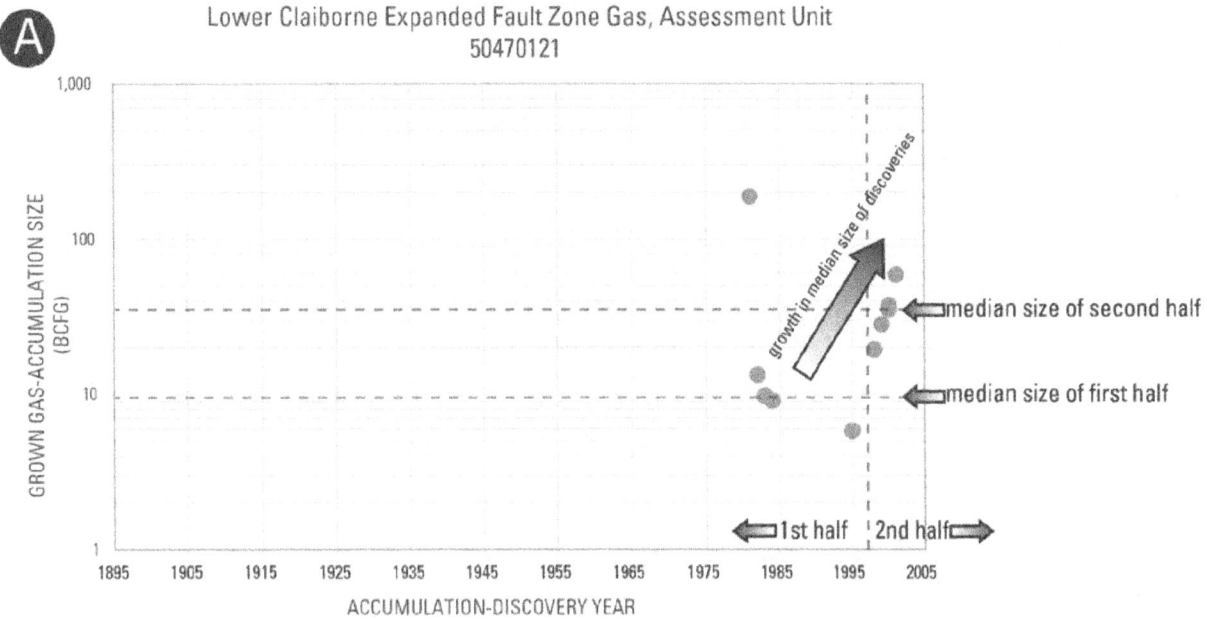

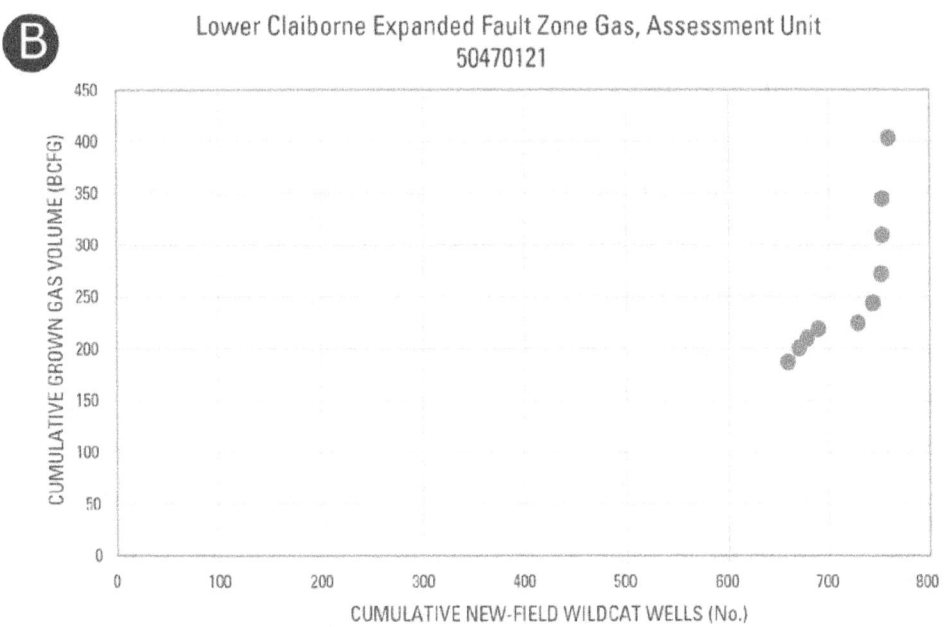

Figure 33. Gas discovery curve and wildcat wells for the Lower Claiborne Expanded Fault Zone assessment unit (AU). A, Grown gas accumulation sizes for the Lower Claiborne Expanded Fault Zone AU (50470121) plotted as a function of discovery year. B, Cumulative grown gas volumes for the Lower Claiborne Expanded Fault Zone AU (50470121) plotted as a function of the cumulative number of new-field wildcat wells. Data from NRG Associates (2006), plotted by T. Klett, USGS. BCFG = billion cubic feet of gas.

1980s. Sizes of undiscovered gas accumulations were estimated to be a minimum of 3 BCFG (minimum cutoff size), a maximum of 700 BCFG, and a median of 20 BCFG. The maximum estimated field size of 700 BCFG is larger (approximately 3.5 times) than the grown size of any field discovered to date. However, the relatively low exploration density and the substantial depth to discovered reservoirs indicate that wide areas of the AU are untested as yet, from which is inferred significant uncertainty in the maximum undiscovered reservoir size. Cumulative discovered gas volumes in the AU show a strong increase as a function of the cumulative number of new field wildcat wells (fig. 33B), hinting at the possibility for large discoveries with additional exploration. Finally, all of the discovered fields in the AU still are in production, indicating the potential for significant reserve growth for as-yet undiscovered reservoirs. The estimated median undiscovered field size of 20 BCGF reflects a decline from the median of the second half of discovered reservoirs (35.1 BCFG). Reservoir depths for gas accumulations also are expected to range between 8,000 and 14,000 ft. Mean estimates of undiscovered resources for the Lower Claiborne Expanded Fault Zone Gas AU from Monte Carlo simulation are 4 MMBO, 1,006 BCFG, and 40 MMBNGL (table 1).

The first discovery in the downdip Queen City was the Mestena Grande field (fig. 31) in 1981. This field and the nine other discovered gas fields in the AU all are deeper than 9,000 ft. Five discoveries have been made in the past decade. All discovered accumulations are overpressured, occur in structural traps, and all currently are in production. An estimated 770 new field wildcat wells penetrate the top of the Yegua in this assessment unit for an approximate high-side exploration density of 1 wildcat for every 4.7 mi^2. However, as pointed out in the previous section, many of these wildcats do not encounter the lower Claiborne section.

The potential for discovery of new gas fields in this AU is high, based on the potential depth to undiscovered reservoirs, overpressured conditions which moderate porosity reduction (Winker, 1982), the relatively low level of exploration, and the fact that more sandstones may be present downdip of the established trends (Schenk and Viger, 1996a). Undiscovered accumulations are expected to be deep gas in structural traps. The expanded reservoir facies will occur in lowstand systems tracts including lowstand deltas, delta front and distal shelf sands, incised valley fill, and upper slope sands.

Lower Claiborne Slope and Basin Floor Gas (50470122)

The Lower Claiborne Slope and Basin Floor Gas AU is located basinward of the other two Lower Claiborne AUs, extending from their southwestern boundaries to the State waters limit (fig. 31). The AU occupies an area of about 15.8 million acres, the great bulk of which is in Texas. The northwestern boundary is defined by the limit of reservoir expansion as determined by sand input to the Lower Claiborne Expanded Fault Zone AU and by the upper Wilcox shelf margin to the northeast of the limit of lower Claiborne progradation. The eastern boundary is defined by the loss of sand influx, and the southeastern boundary is the limit of State waters. At its most northeastern limit, the AU contains about 60,000 acres in Louisiana. This is a somewhat liberal consideration, as most sand input during lower Claiborne time occurred in the area of the Rio Grande Embayment. A more conservative drawing of the boundary may limit the eastward limit of the AU to the area west of Bee County (fig. 31), as suggested above for the Lower Claiborne Expanded Fault Zone Gas AU (T.E. Ewing, Frontera Exploration Consultants, Inc., written commun., 2008).

The Lower Claiborne Slope and Basin Floor Gas AU does not contain any discovered hydrocarbon reservoirs greater than the minimum cutoff of 0.5 MMBO (NRG Associates, 2006) and therefore is considered hypothetical in nature. However, the AU was defined and quantitatively assessed because of the high probability for the existence of undiscovered gas accumulations, due to the inferred presence of adequate source rocks, reservoirs, and the favorable timing of geologic events. The AU is not expected to contain any undiscovered oil accumulations, due to high thermal maturity. The Lower Miocene Slope and Basin Gas AU (50470141) and its Federal offshore extension and a scaled-down Wilcox Slope and Basin Floor Gas AU (50470118) (see Dubiel and others, 2007) were used as analogs to estimate the number and sizes of undiscovered gas accumulations for the Lower Claiborne Slope and Basin Floor Gas AU.

Numbers of undiscovered gas accumulations were estimated to be a minimum of 1, a maximum of 200, and a mode of 20. The maximum number of 200 accumulations was selected because of the relatively large size of the AU (15.8 million acres) and the absence of significant exploration to date. Sizes of undiscovered gas accumulations were estimated to be a minimum of 3 BCFG (minimum cutoff size), a maximum of 1,500 BCFG, and a median of 20 BCFG. Great uncertainty in resource potential because of the absence of significant exploration activity resulted in selection of the maximum size of 1,500 BCFG for undiscovered accumulations. The presence of multiple discovered 100+ BCFG fields in the downdip upper Claiborne also points to the potential for large undiscovered reservoirs in the downdip environments of the lower Claiborne. Reservoir depths are expected to range between 12,000 and 30,000 ft. There is some overlap in the depth range of undiscovered reservoirs with the Lower Claiborne Expanded Fault Zone AU (50470121) to reflect the as-yet unexplored nature of the boundary between the two environments at around 12,000 to 14,000 ft. Mean estimates of undiscovered resources for the Lower Claiborne Slope and Basin Floor Gas AU from Monte Carlo simulation are 3,620 BCFG and 145 MMBNGL (table 1).

Recent Wilcox discoveries in the deep water Gulf of Mexico attest to the potential for offshelf Paleogene hydrocarbon reservoirs in the Gulf Basin (French and others, 2006). Such basin blanket turbidite fan sandstones may have been delivered via incised canyon sediment conduits from the contemporary shelf margin (McDonnell and others, 2008). However, despite the presence of high-quality Wilcox reservoirs, work in the deepwater Gulf of Mexico illustrates a sand-poor Claiborne section in the distal offshelf downdip environment (Meyer and others, 2005). Exploration wells in the area of Wharton and Victoria Counties (fig. 31), which penetrated the top of Wilcox, did not find sand in the lower Claiborne, indicating either that no sand was delivered or that shelf bypass in this area resulted in nondeposition of reservoir facies (T.E. Ewing, Frontera Exploration Consultants, Inc., written commun., 2008). However, in south Texas, no significant exploration has penetrated the lower Claiborne section, and the presence of lowstand sands is entirely speculative.

An estimated 860 new field wildcat wells penetrate the top of the Yegua in this assessment unit for an approximate high-side exploration density of 1 wildcat well for every 28.7 mi^2. However, within the bounds of the AU there are no wells coded for lower Claiborne production in the IHS database, suggesting that the great majority (probably >95 percent, T.E. Ewing, Frontera Exploration Consultants, Inc., written commun., 2008) of the new field wildcats do not actually penetrate the top of the Claiborne. The potential for undiscovered hydrocarbon accumulations in this AU is expected to be moderate to high, based on the potential for sand delivery downdip to thin, dispersed reservoirs in distal lowstand systems tracts including mid-lower slope fans, turbidites, basin-floor fans, and distal gravity slide features. Reservoir quality may be a risk factor because of great burial depth (Dutton and Loucks, 2008), but overpressured conditions may preserve porosity for dry gas accumulations occurring in structural traps associated with growth faults that sole out from the deposition of younger overlying strata. There are approximately 180 discovered Expanded Fault Zone Vicksburg reservoirs in structural traps overlying this AU;

projection of these structures to depth could result in discoveries in the hypothetical Lower Claiborne Slope and Basin Floor Gas AU. As described by Ewing and Fergeson (1991), downdip reservoirs in the upper Claiborne Yegua were discovered by drilling on structures projected from the overlying Frio.

Lower Claiborne Cane River (50470123)

The boundaries of the Lower Claiborne Cane River AU are defined on the west at the limit of the other three Lower Claiborne AUs, on the south by the State waters boundary, and on the east by the petroleum province boundary (fig. 31). On the north the boundary is limited by outcrop and (or) the downdip limit of freshwater (freshwater contains <10,000 milligrams/liter total dissolved solids; Pettijohn, 1996). The downdip limit of freshwater was used to define in places the updip boundaries of the Lower Claiborne Cane River AU and the overlying Upper Claiborne Stable Shelf Gas and Oil AU (50470124), because the presence of meteoric water appears to retard biogenic methane generation in coal beds of the Wilcox Group (Warwick, 2004; Warwick and others, 2008). The AU encompasses an area of about 50 million acres. The Lower Claiborne Cane River AU does not contain any discovered hydrocarbon reservoirs greater than the minimum cutoff of 0.5 MMBO (NRG Associates, 2006) and was not assessed on a quantitative basis. An estimated 18,300 new field wildcat wells penetrate the top of the Yegua in this assessment unit, for an approximate high-side exploration density of 1 wildcat well for every 4.2 mi^2.

In east-central Louisiana, approximately 75 wells are coded for past and present hydrocarbon production from the Cane River Formation (IHS Energy Group, 2005a); however, conversations and correspondence with industry representatives indicated that the wells in question were producing from upper sands of the Wilcox Group. Evaluation of the spatial distribution of a subset of these wells and their perforated depths confirmed that they are located in Wilcox oil fields and are perforated at depths conforming to Wilcox sands. Furthermore, previous workers have established that the lower Claiborne Group in the eastern Gulf of Mexico is constituted by thin shales deposited on an open muddy shelf, far from sand distribution centers (Guevara and García, 1972; Payne, 1972; Galloway and others, 2000). Based on the data contained in the NRG Associates (2006) and IHS Energy Group databases (2005a, b), the high exploration density for underlying Wilcox targets, and the paucity of sandy facies, the Lower Claiborne Cane River AU is deemed a poor prospect for undiscovered conventional hydrocarbon accumulations. The potential for autogenic shale gas currently is unknown but herein is considered poor due to low Claiborne thermal maturity north of the Wilcox shelf break. The Lower Claiborne Cane River AU may be thermally mature for gas generation at depth south of the Wilcox shelf break; however, great drilling depths, the expected minimal thickness (or absence of the Claiborne section, O'Donnell, 1974; Dockery, 1976), and unknown fracturing character may preclude exploration for shale gas systems in the near future.

Upper Claiborne Stable Shelf Gas and Oil (50470124)

The Upper Claiborne Stable Shelf Gas and Oil AU has the largest areal extent of all Claiborne Group assessment units, extending from the international border in south Texas to Escambia County in the Florida panhandle (fig. 34) and encompassing an area of approximately 50.4 million acres. The AU boundary is defined by the international boundary on the southwest and by outcrop on the north and west. Outcrop was used as the boundary on the north and west to account for some very shallow Texas oil production (IHS Energy Group, 2005a). The northeastern boundary is defined by the limits of scattered production in the Mississippi Embayment and by the

54

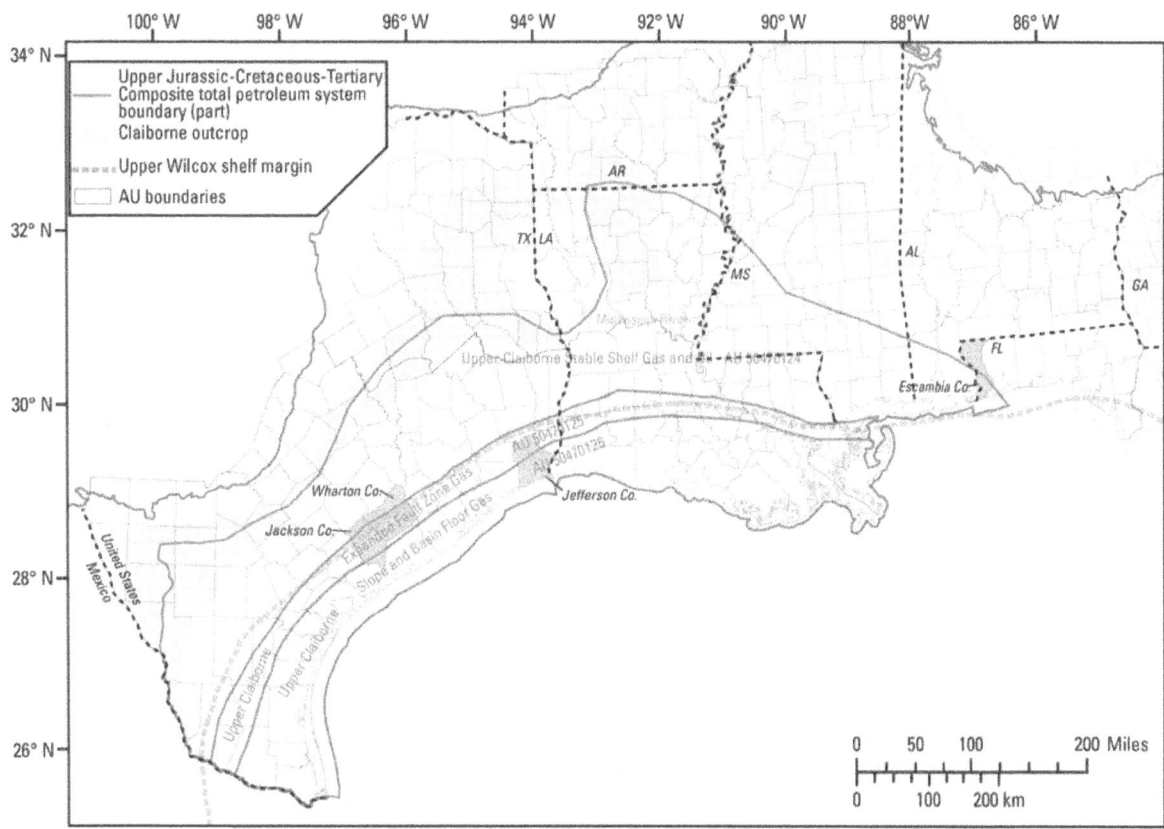

Figure 34. Map showing extent of upper Claiborne assessment units (AU). Claiborne Group outcrop is from Schruben and others (1994); Wilcox Group shelf margin is from Galloway and others (2000). Co. = County. Locations/counties noted on figure are referred to in the text.

downdip limit of freshwater (Pettijohn, 1996) on the northeast. As described above, the downdip limit of freshwater was used as the boundary on the northeast to account for the possibility of shallow biogenic gas production. (Coal beds are present in the updip, terrestrial Claiborne section, Hackley and others, 2006.) The southeastern boundary is defined by the State water limit. The southern boundary in Louisiana is defined by the underlying relict Wilcox shelf margin, as there was no or very little shelf margin progradation in this area according to the interpretations of Galloway and others (2000). In Texas, the southern boundary is defined by the approximate underlying Wilcox shelf edge and the updip limit of the upper Claiborne expansion zone.

The Upper Claiborne Stable Shelf Gas and Oil AU is an established exploration and production trend with 175 oil and 153 gas accumulations that exceed the minimum size considered for this assessment (0.5 MMBO and 3 BCFG for oil and gas accumulations, respectively). The median grown sizes of discovered gas accumulations, when divided into thirds (by early, middle, and late initial dates of production), are 14.5, 7.1, and 8.7 BCFG (fig. 27), respectively, and for discovered oil accumulations are 2.1, 1.7, and 1.2 MMBO (fig. 35A), respectively. The slight growth in median gas thirds between the second and third one-third is interpreted to represent spatial overlap between this AU and the downdip Upper Claiborne Expanded Fault Zone Gas AU (50470125), which has been developed more recently. The decline in median oil accumulation sizes indicates that this AU is mature for oil exploration. Grown discovered gas accumulations total 10.09 TCFG and grown discovered oil accumulations total 1,660 MMBO. The AU was considered

55

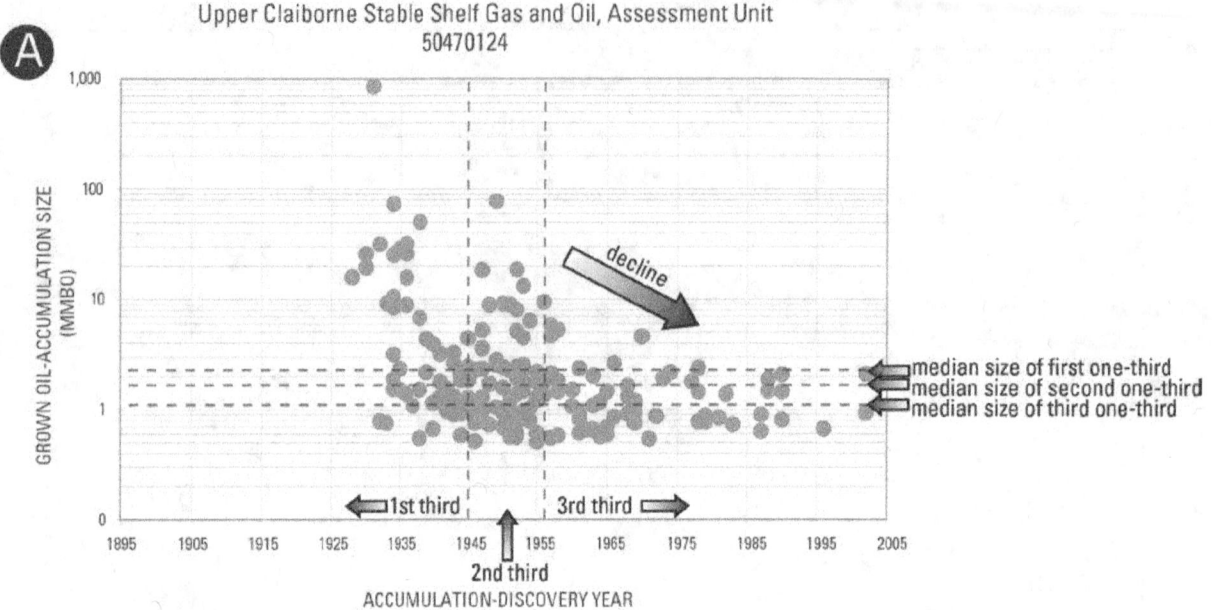

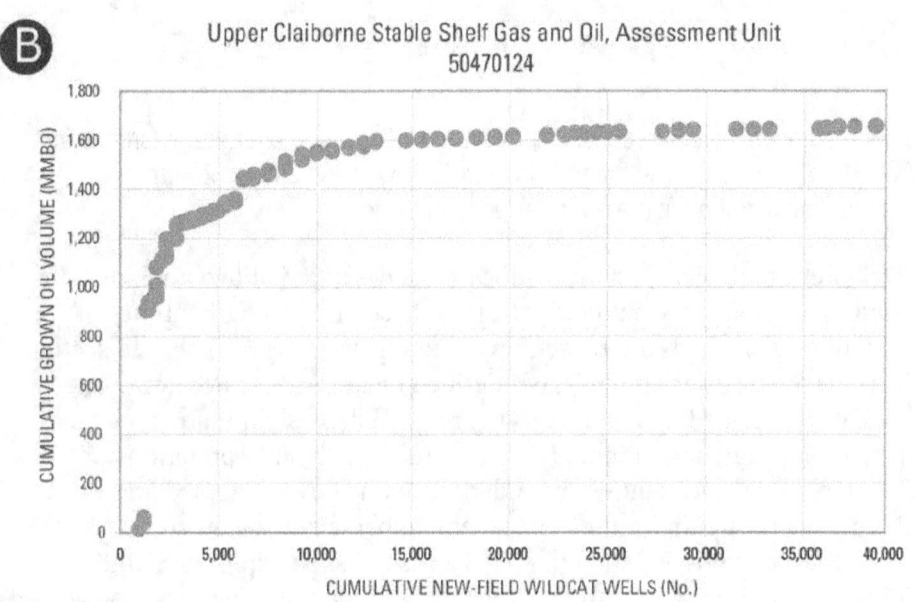

Figure 35. Oil discovery curve and wildcat wells for the Upper Claiborne Stable Shelf Gas and Oil assessment unit (AU). A, Grown oil accumulation sizes for the Upper Claiborne Stable Shelf Gas and Oil AU (50470124) plotted as a function of discovery year. B, Cumulative grown oil volumes for the Upper Claiborne Stable Shelf Gas and Oil AU (50470124) plotted as a function of the cumulative number of new-field wildcat wells. Data from NRG Associates (2006), plotted by T. Klett, USGS. MMBO = million barrels of oil.

to contain one or more undiscovered hydrocarbon accumulations on the basis of having adequate charge, reservoir rocks, and favorable timing of geologic events.

The number of undiscovered oil accumulations is estimated to be a minimum of 1, a maximum of 30, and a mode of 10. The maximum and mode numbers were selected to account for the fact that although this is a highly mature area in terms of exploration, it also is a vast AU in terms of total area, and therefore there is some potential for the presence of undiscovered oil reservoirs, particularly in the less-explored downdip and deeper parts of the AU. Sizes of oil accumulations were estimated to be a minimum of 0.5 MMBO (minimum cutoff size), a maximum of 5 MMBO, and a median of 0.8 MMBO. The size of fields discovered in the AU over the last 50 years is relatively constant, ranging between 0.5 and 10 MMBO (fig. 35A); the maximum size of 5 MMBO for undiscovered fields was selected to allow for the possibility that this consistent discovery trend would continue into the future. The median size of 0.8 MMBO was selected to account for decline from the last third of median discovered field sizes (1.2 MMBO) and to be consistent with data indicating that additional exploration will likely add little to cumulative discovered oil volumes (fig. 35B).

Numbers of undiscovered gas accumulations were estimated to be a minimum of 4, a maximum of 75, and a mode of 15. Although this is a mature area in terms of exploration, it is a very large area, and the maximum and mode for undiscovered gas accumulations were chosen to reflect that the downdip and deeper parts of the AU have good potential for new discoveries. In addition, exploration for deeper objectives using 3-D seismic at the downdip margin of the AU has resulted in the discovery of many new reservoirs since the 1980s. Sizes of undiscovered gas accumulations were estimated to be a minimum of 3 BCFG (minimum cutoff size), a maximum of 400 BCFG, and a median of 6 BCFG. The maximum size estimate of 400 BCFG was selected because there are multiple discovered 100+ BCFG reservoirs in this AU (fig. 27), as well as recently discovered (post-2000) reservoirs of similar size in the downdip Upper Claiborne Expanded Fault Zone AU (50470125). The median size of 6 BCFG was selected as being consistent with the median size of the discoveries made in the past three decades.

Reservoir depths for undiscovered oil and gas accumulations are expected to range between 1,000 and 11,400 ft. The relatively greater lower cutoff depth used for this AU is to account for greater subsidence on the Louisiana shelf and the resultant thick Oligocene-Miocene section in this area. In particular, some of the deep (>10,000 ft) Sparta reservoirs in Louisiana are in the stable shelf environment despite being several thousand feet deeper than the 8,000 ft cutoff used in the previously described analysis of the geologic model used for this assessment. Mean estimates of undiscovered resources from Monte Carlo simulation for the Upper Claiborne Stable Shelf Gas and Oil AU are 13 MMBO, 442 BCFG, and 12 MMBNGL (table 1).

An estimated 40,000 new field wildcat wells penetrate the top of the Yegua in this AU, for an approximate high-side exploration density of 1 wildcat well per every 2.0 mi^2. The potential for new discoveries in thin highstand and transgressive systems tract reservoir sands in the fluvial, deltaic, delta mouth, strandline-barrier bar, and proximal shelf environments on the stable shelf is expected to be low due to the high level of exploration. Undiscovered accumulations probably are deep gas in structural traps near the basinward margin of the AU and possibly some small oil accumulations in subtle, shallow stratigraphic traps.

Upper Claiborne Expanded Fault Zone Gas (50470125)

The Upper Claiborne Expanded Fault Zone Gas AU is located basinward of the contemporary updip Upper Claiborne Stable Shelf Gas and Oil AU and extends from the international border to Mississippi State waters (fig. 34). The AU encompasses an area of about 9.0 million acres. The boundary on the north and west is defined by the southern limit of the Upper Claiborne Stable Shelf Gas and Oil AU, which is controlled by the shelf margin of the underlying strata. In south to central Texas, the underlying shelf margin is defined by the limit of lower Claiborne Queen City progradation. In easternmost Texas and continuing east into Louisiana there was little or no Claiborne progradation (less toward the east), and the assessment unit brackets the underlying Wilcox shelf margin. The AU boundary on the south and southeast is the downdip limit of expansion. This typically is below the Vicksburg Fault Zone (T.E. Ewing, Frontera Exploration Consultants, Inc., written commun., 2008) and is the theoretical updip limit of the overlying Vicksburg Expanded Fault Zone AU as described in the geologic model used for this assessment. The eastern boundary is limited by State waters; however, this may be somewhat optimistic, as regional-scale studies have indicated that the expansion zone may not be present east of the Mississippi River, where the Claiborne is very thin and may be partially or completely removed by unconformity (O'Donnell, 1974; Dockery, 1976; T.E. Ewing, Frontera Exploration Consultants, Inc., written commun., 2008).

The Upper Claiborne Expanded Fault Zone Gas AU is an established exploration and production trend with 11 oil and 97 gas accumulations that exceed the minimum size considered in this assessment (0.5 MMBO and 3 BCFG for oil and gas accumulations, respectively). About 25 discoveries have been made in the last 10 years (NRG Associates, 2006). The median grown sizes of discovered gas accumulations, when divided into thirds (by early, middle, and late initial dates of production), are 23.5, 23.5, and 25.6 BCFG (fig. 36A), respectively, and for discovered oil accumulations (halves), are 2.4 and 1.9 MMBO, respectively. The similarity in median gas thirds is interpreted to represent spatial overlap between this AU and the updip Upper Claiborne Stable Shelf Gas and Oil AU (50470124), which has had a much longer development history. Total grown discovered gas resources are 3.9 TCFG; total grown oil resources are 41.3 MMBO. This AU was considered to contain one or more undiscovered hydrocarbon accumulations on the basis of having adequate charge, reservoir rocks, and favorable timing of geologic events.

The number of undiscovered oil accumulations is estimated to be a minimum of 1, a maximum of 40, and a mode of 10. The maximum of 40 was selected because the deep distal parts of the AU are still frontier and essentially are an untested trend with many areas yet to be drilled. The mode of 10 was selected because this is an overall gas- and condensate-prone AU. Sizes of oil accumulations were estimated to be a minimum of 0.5 MMBO (minimum cutoff size), a maximum of 5 MMBO, and a median of 1.5 MMBO. At the maximum, 5 MMBO was selected to allow for the possibility of an undiscovered field 25 percent of the size of the largest discovered oil field in the AU. The median of 1.5 MMBO was selected to account for decline from the median size of the second half of discovered fields (1.9 MMBO).

Numbers of undiscovered gas accumulations were estimated to be a minimum of 10, a maximum of 360, and a mode of 90. As with oil accumulations, the relatively high mode and maximum of undiscovered gas accumulations were assigned on the basis of the unexplored nature of the downdip and deeper parts of the AU, as well as because of its regional extent. Sizes of undiscovered gas accumulations were estimated to be a minimum of 3 BCFG (minimum cutoff size), a maximum of 400 BCFG, and a median of 20 BCFG. The 400 BCFG estimated maximum is based on the presence of multiple 100+ BCFG recently discovered fields, as well as continuing growth of cumulative discovered gas volumes with exploration (fig. 36B). The median of 20 BCFG is consistent with the recent trend in discovery size.

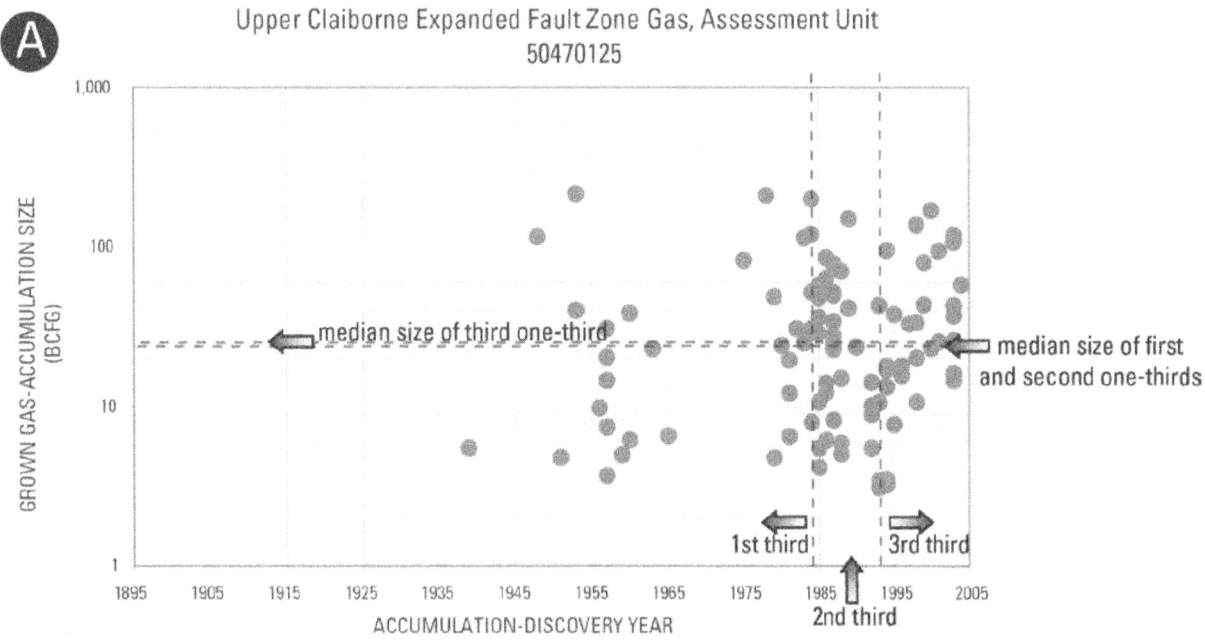

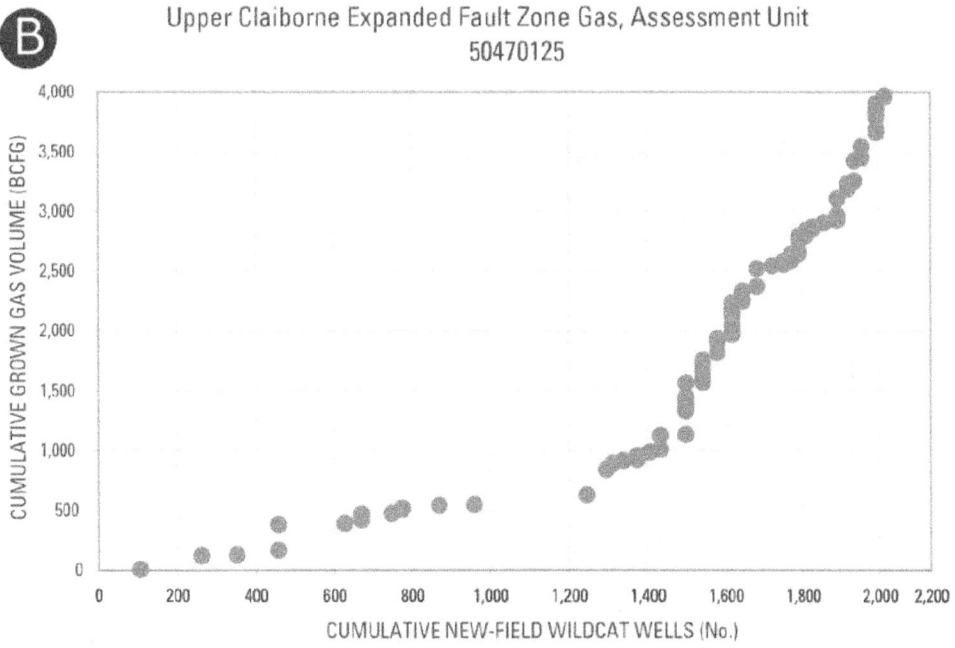

Figure 36. Gas discovery curve and wildcat wells for the Upper Claiborne Expanded Fault Zone assessment unit (AU). A, Grown gas accumulation sizes for the Upper Claiborne Expanded Fault Zone AU (50470125) plotted as a function of discovery year. B, Cumulative grown gas volumes for the Upper Claiborne Expanded Fault Zone AU (50470125) plotted as a function of the cumulative number of new-field wildcat wells. Data from NRG Associates (2006), plotted by T. Klett, USGS. BCFG = billion cubic feet of gas.

Depths of undiscovered reservoirs are expected to range between 5,000 and 14,000 ft for oil accumulations and 5,000 and 16,000 ft for gas accumulations. The shallower cutoff of 5,000 ft (as opposed to 8,000 ft used in the analysis of the geologic model) is to include the possibility that some reservoirs deposited in the expanded fault zone environment have been brought shallower by salt diapirism, particularly in the Houston Embayment. Mean estimates of undiscovered resources from Monte Carlo simulation for the Upper Claiborne Expanded Fault Zone Gas AU are 28 MMBO, 4,882 BCFG, and 351 MMBNGL (table 1).

An estimated 2,040 new field wildcats penetrate the top of the Yegua in this AU for an approximate high-side exploration density of 1 wildcat well per every 6.9 mi^2. The AU is considered to have a high potential for new discoveries, primarily deep gas occurring in structural traps associated with contemporary growth-expansion faults. The relatively low exploration density implies that expanded reservoir sands in lowstand systems tracts including lowstand deltas, delta front and distal shelf sands, incised valley fill, and upper slope sands remain to be found. Overpressured conditions may preserve porosity for non-associated gas and condensate accumulations. Most new downdip Yegua wells flow 1–5 MMCFG/day with 35–500 barrels condensate (Ewing and Fergeson, 1991), and some wells in Jefferson County, Tex. (fig. 34), flow as much as 30 MMCFG/day (T.E. Ewing, Frontera Exploration Consultants, Inc., written commun., 2008). However, the prediction of sand reservoirs in the downdip Yegua has proved difficult, and this interval is composed mainly of shales in many exploration wells along the Texas coast (Swenson, 1997). Nonetheless, thick, high-quality downdip Yegua sands are present, interspersed with thick marine shales; in some areas thinner, high-quality sands as well as laminated sands are present with shales (Swenson, 1997; Ewing and Vincent, 1997b; T.E. Ewing, Frontera Exploration Consultants, Inc., written commun., 2008). Swenson (1997) postulated that an oversteepened shelf edge break northeast of the Jackson-Wharton County area may have caused shelf margin bypass of Yegua sands to slope mini-basins and basin floor fans. If this is the case, sand reservoirs would be present even farther downdip in the Upper Claiborne Slope and Basin Floor Gas AU (50470126). The precise nature and location of the boundary between the expanded fault zone and the slope and basin floor environments have not been completely revealed by exploration to date, although some discovered reservoir sands in the expanded fault zone are representative of upper slope environments (T.E. Ewing, Frontera Exploration Consultants, Inc., written commun., 2008).

Upper Claiborne Slope and Basin Floor Gas (50470126)

The Upper Claiborne Slope and Basin Floor Gas AU lies basinward of the contemporary upper Claiborne expansion zone (fig. 34). The AU encompasses an area of about 22.8 million acres. The boundary on the north and west is defined by the southern boundary of AU 50470125 (the theoretical updip limit of Vicksburg expansion), and on the south and east by the State waters boundary.

The Upper Claiborne Slope and Basin Floor Gas AU does not contain any discovered hydrocarbon reservoirs greater than the minimum cutoff of 0.5 MMBO (NRG Associates, 2006) and therefore is considered hypothetical in nature. However, the AU was defined and quantitatively assessed because of the high probability for the existence of undiscovered gas accumulations greater than the minimum size cutoff, due to the inferred presence of adequate source rocks, reservoir rocks, and the favorable timing of geologic events. No oil accumulations are expected for this AU, due to high thermal maturity. The Lower Miocene Slope and Basin Gas AU (50470141) and its Federal offshore extension AU and a scaled-down Wilcox Slope and Basin Floor Gas AU

(50470118; Dubiel and others, 2007) were used as analogs for estimating the numbers and sizes of undiscovered gas accumulations in the Upper Claiborne Slope and Basin Floor Gas AU.

Contact with industry personnel (2006–2008) indicates that there currently is no production from the slope and basin floor environments of the Claiborne downdip of the expanded fault zone. However, deep wells have encountered sands in the Claiborne section out to nearly the present shoreline (T.E. Ewing, Frontera Exploration Consultants, Inc., written commun., 2008). Despite the presence of sand, lack of sufficient gas charge has been a problem in making these exploration wells economic to date, possibly due to salt movement and trap disruption (T.E. Ewing, Frontera Exploration Consultants, Inc., written commun., 2008).

Numbers of undiscovered gas accumulations in the Upper Claiborne Slope and Basin Floor AU were estimated to be a minimum of 5, a maximum of 500, and a mode of 50. The maximum of 500 was selected because of the vast size of the AU and the absence of significant exploration to date. The mode of 50 was scaled down from Wilcox and Miocene analogs, due to lower volumes of sand delivery. Sizes of undiscovered gas accumulations were estimated to be a minimum of 3 BCFG (minimum cutoff size), a maximum of 1,500 BCFG, and a median of 20 BCFG. The maximum size of 1,500 BCFG was selected because of the high degree of uncertainty in this frontier environment and because of the presence of multiple 100+ BCFG discovered reservoirs in the updip Upper Claiborne Expanded Fault Zone AU (50470125). Depths to undiscovered gas accumulations are expected to range between 12,000 and 30,000 ft. As described for the lower Claiborne, the boundary between the expanded fault zone and the slope and basin floor environment has not been explored, and therefore the predicted depth to undiscovered accumulations overlaps between this AU and the updip Upper Claiborne Expanded Fault Zone AU (50470125). Mean estimates of undiscovered resources from Monte Carlo simulation for the Upper Claiborne Slope and Basin Floor Gas AU are 9,107 BCFG and 655 MMBNGL (table 1).

An estimated 820 new field wildcats penetrate the top of the Yegua in this AU for an approximate high-side exploration density of 1 wildcat well per every 43.7 mi^2. Approximately 20 wells in the AU are coded for upper Claiborne production in the IHS database. However, conversations and correspondence with industry personnel (2006–2008) indicate that at least some of the wells in question are in fact producing from younger intervals and therefore are miscoded. Based on this information, it is assumed that the exploration density is even lower than predicted by the high-side new field wildcat exercise. The potential for new discoveries in this AU is expected to be very high due to the very low level of exploration and the inferred presence of adequate reservoir rocks in distal lowstand systems tracts including mid-lower slope fans, turbidites, basin-floor fans, and distal gravity slide features. As described above for the Lower Claiborne Slope and Basin Floor Gas AU (50470122), reservoir quality may be a risk factor although it is expected that overpressured conditions would preserve porosity for dry gas accumulations. Undiscovered reservoirs primarily would be in structural traps associated with the growth faults that sole out from the deposition of overlying strata. Given current high natural gas prices, instability of world markets, and renewed interest in developing domestic supplies, we expect that significant resources will be devoted by Gulf of Mexico operators in the coming decades to the exploration and production of overpressured downdip gas accumulations in the Claiborne Group and in the other Cenozoic clastic packages described in this volume.

References Cited

Ahlbrandt, T.S., 2000, Introduction, *in* U.S. Geological Survey world petroleum assessment 2000—Description and results: U.S. Geological Survey Digital Data Series DDS-60, version 1.0, 4 CD-ROMs.

Allison, A.P., Beckelhymer, R.L., Benson, D.G., Hutchins, R.M., Jr., Lake, C.L., Lewis, R.C., O'Bannon, P.H., Self, S.R., and Warner, C.A., 1946, Geology of Katy field, Waller, Harris, and Fort Bend Counties, Texas: American Association of Petroleum Geologists Bulletin, v. 30, no. 2, p. 157–180.

American Oil and Gas Historical Society, 2005, Technology solves Conroe: The Petroleum Age, v. 2, no. 2, p. 8–10.

Attanasi, E.D., and Root, D.H., 1994, The enigma of oil and gas field growth: American Association of Petroleum Geologists Bulletin, v. 78, no. 3, p. 321–332.

Barker, C.E., and Pawlewicz, M.J., 1986, The correlation of vitrinite reflectance with maximum temperature in humic organic matter, *in* Buntebarth, G., and Stegena, L., eds., Paleogeothermics, Lecture Notes in Earth Science 5: Berlin, Springer, p. 79–93.

Bebout, D.G., and Gutiérrez, D.R., 1982, Regional cross sections, Louisiana Gulf coast (western part): Louisiana Geological Survey Folio Series No. 5, 11 p.

Bebout, D.G., and Gutiérrez, D.R., 1983, Regional cross sections, Louisiana Gulf coast (eastern part): Louisiana Geological Survey Folio Series No. 6, 10 p.

Bouma, A.H., 1962, Sedimentology of some flysch deposits: a graphic approach to facies interpretation: Amsterdam, Elsevier Publishing Company, 168 p.

Buffler, R.T., 1991, Early evolution of the Gulf of Mexico basin, *in* Goldthwaite, D., ed., Introduction to central Gulf Coast geology: New Orleans Geological Society, p. 1–15.

Burnett, R.C., 1990, Seismic amplitude anomalies and AVO analyses at Mestena Grande field, Jim Hogg County, Texas: Geophysics, v. 55, no. 8, p. 1015–1025.

Cathles, L.M., 2004, Hydrocarbon generation, migration, and venting in a portion of the offshore Louisiana Gulf of Mexico basin: The Leading Edge, p. 760–770.

Charpentier, R.R., and Klett, T.R., 2005, A Monte Carlo simulation method for the assessment of undiscovered, conventional oil and gas, *in* USGS Southwestern Wyoming Province Assessment Team, compilers, Petroleum systems and geologic assessment of oil and gas in the southwestern Wyoming province, Wyoming, Colorado and Utah: U.S. Geological Survey Digital Data Series DDS-69-D, chapter 21, 5 p., accessed November 4, 2008 at *http://certmapper.cr.usgs.gov/data/noga00/natl/text/CH_21.pdf*.

Claypool, G.E., and Mancini, E.A., 1989, Geochemical relationships of petroleum in Mesozoic reservoirs to carbonate source rocks of Jurassic Smackover Formation: American Association of Petroleum Geologists Bulletin, v. 73, p. 904–924.

Condon, S.M., and Dyman, T.S., 2006, 2003 geologic assessment of undiscovered conventional oil and gas resources in the Upper Cretaceous Navarro and Taylor Groups, Western Gulf Province, Texas: U.S. Geological Survey Digital Data Series DDS–69–H, Chapter 2, 42 p., accessed August 15, 2007, at *http://pubs.usgs.gov/dds/dds-069/dds-069-h/REPORTS/69_H_CH_2.pdf*.

Cooke, C.W., 1918, Correlation of the deposits of Jackson and Vicksburg ages in Mississippi and Alabama: Washington Academy of Sciences Journal, v. 8, p. 186–198.

Davies, D.K., and Ethridge, F.G., 1971, The Claiborne Group of central Texas: a record of Middle Eocene marine and coastal plain deposition: Gulf Coast Association of Geological Societies Transactions, v. 21, p. 119–128.

Dickinson, G., 1953, Geological aspects of abnormal reservoir pressures in Gulf Coast Louisiana: American Association of Petroleum Geologists Bulletin, v. 37, p. 410–432.

Dockery, D.T., III, 1976, Depositional systems in the upper Claiborne and lower Jackson groups (Eocene) of Mississippi: University of Mississippi, M.S. thesis, 110 p.

Dodge, M.M., and Posey, J.S., 1981, Structural cross sections, Tertiary formations, Texas Gulf Coast: Bureau of Economic Geology, University of Texas at Austin, Department of Energy Contract DE-AC08-78ET11397, 32 plates.

Dow, W.G., 1977, Kerogen studies and geological interpretations: Journal of Geochemical Exploration, v. 7, p. 79–99.

Dow, W.G., 1984, Oil source beds and oil prospect definition in the upper Tertiary of the Gulf Coast: Gulf Coast Association of Geological Societies Transactions, v. 34, p. 329–339.

Dubiel R.F., Pitman, J.K., Pearson, O.N., Warwick, P.D., Karlsen, A.W., Coleman, J.L., Hackley, P.C., Hayba, D.O., Swanson, S.M., Charpentier, R.R., Cook, T.A., Klett, T.R., Pollastro, R.M., and Schenk, C.J., 2007, Assessment of undiscovered oil and gas resources in Tertiary strata of the Gulf Coast, 2007: U.S. Geological Survey Fact Sheet FS-2007-3066, 4 p. accessed July 2, 2012, at *http://pubs.usgs.gov/fs/2007/3066/*.

Dutton, S.P., and Loucks, R.G., 2008, Controls on evolution of porosity and permeability in lower Tertiary Wilcox Sandstones from 200 to 6700 meters of burial: 33rd International Geological Congress, Oslo, Norway, Aug. 6–14, 2008, Abstract 1210439, unpaginated, CD-ROM.

Eargle, D.H., 1968, Nomenclature of formations of Claiborne Group, Middle Eocene coastal plain of Texas: U.S. Geological Survey Bulletin 1251-D, 25 p.

Echols, J.B., Zimmerman, R.K., and Goddard, D.A., 1994, An integrated geochemical and geological approach for determining hydrocarbon generation-migration patterns: central Gulf Coast basin: Gulf Coast Association of Geological Societies Transactions, v. 44, p. 193–203.

Edwards, M.B., 1991, Control of depositional environments, eustasy, gravity, and salt tectonics on sandstone distribution in an unstable shelf edge delta, Eocene Yegua Formation, Texas and Louisiana: Gulf Coast Association of Geological Societies Transactions, v. 41, p. 237–252.

Eguiluz de Antuñano, S., 2001, Geologic evolution and gas resources of the Sabinas Basin in northeastern Mexico, *in* Bartolini, C., Buffler, R.T., and Cantú-Chapa, A., eds., The western Gulf of Mexico Basin: Tectonics, sedimentary basins, and petroleum systems: American Association of Petroleum Geologists Memoir 75, p. 241–270.

Evans, R., 1987, Pathways of migration of oil and gas in the south Mississippi Salt Basin: Gulf Coast Association of Geological Societies Transactions, v. 37, p. 75–85.

Eversull, L.G., 1984, Regional cross sections, north Louisiana: Louisiana Geological Survey Folio Series No. 7, 11 p.

Ewing, T.E., 1983, Growth faults and salt tectonics in the Houston diapir province: relative timing and exploration significance: Gulf Coast Association of Geological Societies Transactions, v. 33, p. 83–90.

Ewing, T.E., 1991, Structural framework, *in* Salvador, A., ed., The Gulf of Mexico Basin: Boulder, Colo., Geological Society of America, The Geology of North America, v. J, p. 31–52.

Ewing, T.E., 1994, The Cook Mountain problem: stratigraphic reality and semantic confusion: Gulf Coast Association of Geological Societies Transactions, v. 44, p. 225–232.

Ewing, T.E., 2001, Shanghai field, expanded upper Yegua trend, Texas Gulf Coast: Unexpected reserves and a distinctive fault style defined by 3D seismic: Houston Geological Society Bulletin, v. 44, no. 2, p. 19–25.

Ewing, T.E., 2008, Fairways in the downdip and middle Yegua trend – a review of 25 years of exploration: Bulletin of the South Texas Geological Society, v. 48, no. 6, p. 21–41.

Ewing, T.E., Budnik, R.T., Ames, J.T., Ridner, D.M., and Dillon, R.L., 1990, Tectonic map of Texas: University of Texas at Austin, Bureau of Economic Geology, 4 sheets, scale 1:750,000.

Ewing, T.E., and Fergeson, G., 1991, Stratigraphic framework, structural styles and seismic signatures of downdip Yegua gas-condensate fields, central Wharton County, Texas Gulf Coast: Gulf Coast Association of Geological Societies Transactions, v. 41, p. 255–275.

Ewing, T.E., and Lopez, R.F., compilers, 1991, Principal structural features, Gulf of Mexico Basin, *in* Salvador, A., ed., The Gulf of Mexico Basin: Boulder, Colo., Geological Society of America, Geology of North America, v. J, plate 2, scale 1:2,500,000.

Ewing, T.E., and Vincent, F.S., 1997a, Correlation of Yegua/Cockfield genetic cycles, Texas and Louisiana: Gulf Coast Association of Geological Societies Transactions, v. 47, p. 631–633.

Ewing, T.E., and Vincent, F.S., 1997b, Foundered shelf edges – examples from the Yegua and Frio, Texas and Louisiana: Gulf Coast Association of Geological Societies Transactions, v. 47, p. 149–157.

Fang, J., Sassen, R., Roberts, H., and Nunn, J., 1989, Organic geochemistry of sediments of the deep-water Gulf of Mexico basin: Organic Geochemistry, v. 14, p. 679.

Fiduk, J.C., Weimer, P., Trudgill, B.D., Rowan, M.G., Gale, P.E., Phair, R.L., Korn, B.E., Roberts, G.R., Gafford, W.T., Lowe, R.S., and Queffelec, T.A., 1999, The Perdido Fold Belt, northwestern deep Gulf of Mexico, Part 2: seismic stratigraphy and petroleum systems: American Association of Petroleum Geologists Bulletin, v. 83, no. 4, p. 578–612.

Fillon, R. H., 2001, Late Mesozoic and Cenozoic deposystem evolution in the eastern Gulf of Mexico: implications for hydrocarbon migration, *in* Fillon, R. H., Rosen, N., Weimer, P., Lowrie, A., Pettingill, H., Phair, R. L., Roberts, H. H., and van Hoorn, B., eds., Petroleum systems of deep-water basins: Global and Gulf of Mexico experience: Gulf Coast Section, Society of Economic Paleontologists and Mineralogists Publication on CD-ROM.

Fisher, W.L., 1969, Facies characterization of Gulf Coast delta systems, with some Holocene analogues: Gulf Coast Association of Geological Societies Transactions, v. 19, p. 239–261.

French, L.S., Richardson, G.E., Kazanis, E.G., Montgomery, T.M., Bohannon, C.M., and Gravois, M.P., 2006, Deepwater Gulf of Mexico 2006: America's expanding frontier: Minerals Management Service Outer Continental Shelf Report 2006–022, 144 p.

French, C.D., and Schenk, C.J., 2004, Map showing geology, oil and gas fields, and geologic provinces of the Caribbean Region: U. S. Geological Survey Open-File Report 97–470–K, 1 sheet, CD-ROM, accessed August 27, 2007, at *http://pubs.usgs.gov/of/1997/ofr-97–470/OF97-470K/*.

French, C.D., and Schenk, C.J., 2005, Map showing the geology, oil and gas fields, and geologic provinces of the Gulf of Mexico Region: U.S. Geological Survey Open-File Report 97–470–L, 1 sheet, CD-ROM, accessed August 27, 2007, at *http://pubs.usgs.gov/of/1997/ofr-97–470/OF97-470L/*).

Galloway, W.E., 1989, Genetic stratigraphic sequences in basin analysis II: application to northwest Gulf of Mexico Cenozoic basin: American Association of Petroleum Geologists Bulletin, v. 73, p.143–154.

Galloway, W.E., 2002, Cenozoic evolution of sediment accumulation in deltaic and shore-zone depositional systems, northern Gulf of Mexico basin: Journal of Marine and Petroleum Geology, v. 18, p. 1031–1040.

Galloway, W.E., 2005, Gulf of Mexico basin depositional record of Cenozoic North American drainage basin evolution: Special Publication of the International Association of Sedimentologists No. 35, p. 409–423.

Galloway, W.E., Bebout, D.G., Fisher, W.L., Dunlap, J.B., Jr., Cabrera-Castro, R., Lugo-Rivera, J.E., and Scott, T.M., 1991, Cenozoic, *in* Salvador, A., ed., The Gulf of Mexico Basin: Boulder, Colo., Geological Society of America, The Geology of North America, v. J, p. 245–324.

Galloway, W.E., Ewing, T.E., Garrett, C.M., Tyler, M., and Bebout, D.G., 1983, Atlas of major Texas oil reservoirs: University of Texas at Austin, Bureau of Economic Geology, 139 p.

Galloway, W.E., Ganey-Curry, P.E., Li, X., and Buffler, R.T., 2000, Cenozoic depositional history of the Gulf of Mexico basin: American Association of Petroleum Geologists Bulletin, v. 84, no. 11, p. 1743–1774.

Galloway, W.E., Liu, X., Travis-Neuberger, D., and Xue, L., 1994, Reference high-resolution correlation cross-sections, Paleogene section, Texas Coastal Plain: Bureau of Economic Geology, University of Texas at Austin, 5 plates, 19 p.

Galloway, W.E., and Williams, T.A., 1991, Sediment accumulation rates in time and space: Paleogene genetic stratigraphic sequences of the northwestern Gulf of Mexico basin: Geology, v. 19, p. 986–989.

Gardner, J., 1938, Laredo – a new name for a unit of Cook Mountain age in the Rio Grande region: Washington Academy of Science Journal, v. 28, no. 7, p. 297–298.

Gatenby, G., 2001, Phase changes: a major aspect of deepwater hydrocarbon migration: Gulf Coast Section, Society for Sedimentary Geology Foundation 21st Annual Research Conference, Petroleum Systems of Deepwater Basins, December 2–5, 2001, p. 453–468.

Gautier, D.L., Dolton, G.L., Takahashi, K.I., and Varnes, K.L., eds., 1996, 1995 national assessment of United States oil and gas resources—Results, methodology, and supporting data: U.S. Geological Survey Digital Data Series DDS-30, version 2, 1 CD-ROM, accessed August 7, 2007, at *http://energy.cr.usgs.gov/oilgas/noga/1995.html*.

Geomap, 1995a, Northeast Texas Gulf Coast: Geomap standard executive reference map 312, 1 sheet, scale 1' = 6 miles.

Geomap, 1995b, Southeast Louisiana: Geomap standard executive reference map 304, 1 sheet, scale 1' = 5 miles.

Geomap, 1995c, Southwest Louisiana: Geomap standard executive reference map 303, 1 sheet, scale 1' = 5 miles.

Goldthwaite, D., 1991, Central Gulf Coast stratigraphy, *in* Goldthwaite, D., ed., An introduction to central Gulf Coast geology: New Orleans Geological Society, p.17–30.

Gregory, W.A., Chinn, E.W., Sassen, R., and Hart, G.F., 1991, Fluorescence microscopy of particulate organic matter: Sparta Formation and Wilcox Group, south central Louisiana: Organic Geochemistry, v. 17, p. 1–9.

Guevara, E.H., and García, R., 1972, Depositional systems and oil-gas reservoirs in the Queen City Formation (Eocene), Texas: University of Texas at Austin, Bureau of Economic Geology Geological Circular 72–4, 22 p.

Hackley, P.C., 2008, USGS assessment of undiscovered conventional oil and gas resources, Middle-Upper Eocene Claiborne Group, Gulf of Mexico onshore and State waters, USA: American Association of Petroleum Geologists Search and Discovery Series, 38 p., accessed April 13, 2012, at *http://www.searchanddiscovery.com/documents/2008/08283hackley/index.htm*.

Hackley, P.C., and Ewing, T.E., 2010, Assessment of undiscovered conventional oil and gas resources, onshore Claiborne Group, U.S. part of the Gulf of Mexico Basin: American Association of Petroleum Geologists Bulletin, v. 94, no. 10, p. 1607–1636.

Hackley, P.C., Warwick, P.D., Thomas, R.E., and Nichols, D.J., 2006, A review of the lignite resources of western Tennessee and the Jackson Purchase area, western Kentucky: U.S. Geological Survey Open-File Report 2006–1078, 34 p., accessed June 21, 2012, at *http://pubs.usgs.gov/of/2006/1078/.*

Handbook of Texas Online, 2001, Oil Springs, Texas: Texas State Historical Association web site, accessed January 5, 2007, at *http://www.tsha.utexas.edu/handbook/online/articles/OO/hvo12.html.*

Hardin, G.C., and Clark, W.K., 1968, Gas resources of Eocene producing trend, upper Gulf Coast of Texas, *in* Beebe, B.W., and Curtis, B.F., eds., Natural gases of North America: American Association of Petroleum Geologists Memoir 9, p. 284–294.

Halbouty, T.M., 1979, Salt domes, Gulf region, United States and Mexico, (2d ed.): Houston, Gulf Publishing, 561 p.

Hood, K.C., Wenger, L.M., Gross, O.P., and Harrison, S.C., 2002, Hydrocarbon systems analysis of the northern Gulf of Mexico: Delineation of hydrocarbon migration pathways using seeps and seismic imaging, *in* Schumacher, D., and LeSchack, L.A., eds., Surface exploration case histories: Applications of geochemistry, magnetics, and remote sensing: American Association of Petroleum Geologists Studies in Geology No. 48 and SEG Geophysical Reference Series No. 11, p. 25–40.

Hosman, R.L., 1996, Regional stratigraphy and subsurface geology of Cenozoic deposits, Gulf Coastal Plain, south-central United States: U.S. Geological Survey Professional Paper 1416-G, 35 p.

Hull, R.A., 1995, Shelf-slope break sedimentation and erosion during deposition of the Claiborne Group in Colorado and Wharton Counties, Texas: Gulf Coast Association of Geological Societies Transactions, v. 45, p. 267–274.

Humble Geochemical Services, Geochemical and Environmental Research Group, BEICIP, Inc., and Brame Geosciences, 2002, Petroleum systems of the Gulf of Mexico: prediction of hydrocarbon charge, GOM source rock and oil as asphaltene kinetics in Temispack 2-D basin modeling, Proposal 2002, 16 p., available at *http://www.humble-inc.com/gom2001.htm.*

IHS Energy Group, 2005a [includes data current as of 2005], PI/Dwights Plus US production data: IHS Energy Group, 15 Inverness Way East, D205, Englewood, Colo.

IHS Energy Group, 2005b [includes data current as of 2005], PI/Dwights Plus US well data: IHS Energy Group, 15 Inverness Way East, D205, Englewood, Colo.

James, K.H., 2004, A simple synthesis of Caribbean geology: American Association of Petroleum Geologists Search and Discovery, Article no. 30026, 5 p., accessed August 9, 2007, at *http://www.searchanddiscovery.com/documents/2004/james/index.htm.*

Johnston, J.E., Heinrich, P.V., Lovelace, J.K., McCulloh, R.P., and Zimmerman, R.K., 2000, Stratigraphic charts of Louisiana: Louisiana Geological Survey Folio Series No. 8, 6 p.

Kane, W.G., and Gierhart, G.B., 1935, Areal geology in northeastern Mexico: American Association of Petroleum Geologists Bulletin, v. 19, p. 1357–1388.

Kennedy, W., 1892, A section from Terrell, Kaufman County, to Sabine Pass on the Gulf of Mexico: Texas Geological Survey Annual Report, v. 3, p. 41–125.

Klett, T.R., 2004, Oil and natural gas resource assessment— Classifications and terminology: Encyclopedia of Energy, Volume 4, Amsterdam, Elsevier, Inc., p. 595–605.

Klett, T.R., Schmoker, J.W., and Charpentier, R.R., 2003, U.S. Geological Survey input-data form and operational procedure for the assessment of conventional petroleum accumulations: U.S. Geological Survey Digital Data Series DDS-69-B, version 1.0, 10 p., available at *http://pubs.usgs.gov/dds/dds-069/dds-069-b/REPORTS/Chapter_20.pdf.*

Koons, C.B., Bond, J.G., and Peirce, F.L., 1974, Effects of depositional environment and postdepositional history on chemical composition of lower Tuscaloosa oils: American Association of Petroleum Geologists Bulletin, v. 58, p. 1272–1280.

Kosters, E.C., Bebout, D.G., Seni, S.J., Garett, C.M., Jr., Brown, L.F., Jr., Hamlin, H.S., Dutton, S.P., Ruppel, S.C., Finley, R.J., and Tyler, N., 1989, Atlas of major Texas gas reservoirs: University of Texas at Austin, Bureau of Economic Geology, 161 p.

Krutak, P.R., and Kimbrell, W.C., 1991, Sparta B sandstones (Eocene), Fordoche field, Point Coupee Parish, Louisiana – a compartmentalized, barrier-island oil and gas reservoir: Gulf Coast Association of Geological Societies Transactions, v. 49, p. 383–404.

Laplante, R.E., 1974, Hydrocarbon generation in Gulf Coast Tertiary sediments: American Association of Petroleum Geologists Bulletin, v. 58, p. 1281–1289.

Leach, W., 1993, New exploration enhancements in south Louisiana Tertiary sediments: Oil and Gas Journal, v. 91, p. 83–86.

Lewan, M.D., 2002, New insights on timing of oil and gas generation in the central Gulf Coast interior zone based on hydrous-pyrolysis kinetic parameters: Gulf Coast Association of Geological Societies Transactions, v. 52, p. 607–620.

Lock, B.E., and Voorhies, S.L., 1988, Sequence stratigraphy as a tool for interpretation of the Cockfield/Yegua in southwestern Louisiana: Gulf Coast Association of Geological Societies Transactions, v. 38, p. 123–131.

Lopez, J.A., and Orgeron, S.A., 1995, Salt tectonism of the United States Gulf Coast basin (2d ed.): New Orleans Geological Society Publication, map scale 1:1,524,000.

Losh, S., 1998, Oil migration in a major growth fault: structural analysis of the Pathfinder core, South Eugene Island Block 330, offshore Louisiana: American Association of Petroleum Geologists Bulletin, v. 82, p. 1694–1710.

Macelwane, J.B., 1940, Fifteen years of geophysics: A chapter in the exploration of United States and Canada, 1924–1939: Oil and Gas Journal, v. 38, p. 250–258.

Magoon, L.B., and Dow, W.G., 1994, The petroleum system, *in* Magoon, L.B., and Dow, W.G., eds., The petroleum system-from source to trap: American Association of Petroleum Geologists Memoir 60, p. 3–24.

Mancini, E.A., Goddard, D.A., Aharon, P., and Barnaby, R., 2006, Resource assessment of the in-place and potentially recoverable deep natural gas resource of the onshore interior salt basins, north-central and northeastern Gulf of Mexico: Department of Geological Sciences, University of Alabama, Department of Energy Contract DE-FC26-03NT41875, 173 p.

Mancini, E.A., Puckett, T.M., and Parcell, W.C., 1999, Modeling of the burial and thermal histories of strata in the Mississippi Interior Salt Basin: Gulf Coast Association of Geological Societies Transactions, v. 49, p. 332–341.

Mancini, E.A., and Tew, B.H., 1994, Claiborne-Jackson Group (Eocene) contact in Alabama and Mississippi: Gulf Coast Association of Geological Societies Transactions, v. 44, p. 431–439.

McBride, B.C., 1998, The evolution of allochthonous salt along a megaregional profile across the northern Gulf of Mexico Basin: American Association of Petroleum Geologists Bulletin, v. 82, p. 1037–1054.

McBride, B.C., Rowan, M.G., and Weimer, P., 1998, The evolution of allochthonous salt systems, northern Green Canyon and Ewing Bank (offshore Louisiana), northern Gulf Of Mexico: American Association of Petroleum Geologists Bulletin, v. 82, p. 1013–1036.

McCuen, M.D., and West, M.A., 1998, 3-D exploitation of Nod Mex reservoirs, Phase Four field, Wharton County, Texas, *in* Allen, J.L., Brown, T.S., John, C.J., Lobo, C.F., and Kiatta, H.W., eds., 3-D seismic case histories from the Gulf Coast Basin: Gulf Coast Association of Geological Societies Special Publication, p. 231–238.

McDade, E.C., Sassen, R., Wenger, L., and Cole, G.A., 1993, Identification of organic-rich Lower Tertiary shales as petroleum source rocks, south Louisiana: Gulf Coast Association of Geological Societies Transactions, v. 43, p. 257–267.

McDonnell, A., Loucks, R.G., and Galloway, W.E., 2008, Paleocene to Eocene deep-water slope canyons, western Gulf of Mexico: Further insights for the provenance of deep-water offshore Wilcox Group plays: American Association of Petroleum Geologists Bulletin, v. 92, p. 1169–1189.

Mello, U.T., and Karner, G.D., 1996, Development of sediment overpressure and its effect on thermal maturation: application to the Gulf of Mexico basin: American Association of Petroleum Geologists Bulletin, v. 80, no. 9, p. 1367–1396.

Meyer, D., Zarra, L., Rains, D., Meltz, B., and Hall, T., 2005, Emergence of the Lower Tertiary Wilcox trend in the deepwater Gulf of Mexico: World Oil, v. 226, no. 5, p. 72–77.

Michaux, F.W., Jr., and Buck, E.O., 1936, Conroe oil field, Montgomery County, Texas: American Association of Petroleum Geologists Bulletin, v. 20, no. 6, p. 736–779.

Miller, R.S., 1993, Characteristics of deep-water Yegua sandstones, Texas and Louisiana: Houston Geological Society Bulletin, v. 35, no. 8, p. 8.

Nehring, R., 1991, Oil and gas resources, *in* Salvador, A., ed., The Gulf of Mexico Basin: Boulder, Colo., Geological Society of America, The Geology of North America, v. J, p. 445–493.

Nelson, E.J., Weimer, P., Caldaro-Baird, J., and McBride, B., 2000, Timing of source rock maturation in the northern Gulf of Mexico basin: Results from thermal modeling of a regional profile: Gulf Coast Association of Geological Societies Transactions, v. 50 (L), p. 309–319.

NRG Associates, 2006, [includes data current as of 2004], The significant oil and gas fields of the United States: NRG Associates, Inc., P.O. Box 1655, Colorado Springs, CO 80901.

Nunn, J.A., and Sassen, R., 1986, The framework of hydrocarbon generation and migration, Gulf of Mexico continental slope: Gulf Coast Association of Geological Societies Transactions, v. 36, p. 257–262.

O'Donnell, T.T., 1974, Depositional systems in the lower Claiborne (Eocene) of central Mississippi: University of Mississippi, M.S. thesis, variously paginated.

Paleo-Data, Inc., 1989, Tenroc Regional Geologic Database: Commercial database accessed July 9, 2006, at *http://www.paleodata.com/*.

Palmer, A.R., and Geissman, J., compilers, 1999, 1999 geologic time scale: The Geological Society of America, Product code CTS004, 1 p., available at *http://www.geosociety.org/science/timescale/timescl.pdf*.

Patterson, J.M., 1942, Stratigraphy of Eocene formations between Laredo and Rio Grande City, Texas: American Association of Petroleum Geologists Bulletin, v. 26, p. 256–274.

Payne, J.N., 1972, Hydrologic significance of lithofacies of the Cane River Formation and equivalents of Arkansas, Louisiana, Mississippi, and Texas: U.S. Geological Survey Professional Paper P 569-C, p. C1-C17.

Peel, F., 2007, The setting and possible mechanism of the 2006 Green Canyon seismic event: Offshore Technology Conference Paper 19032, Houston, Texas, April 30-May 3, 2007, 4 p.

Pettijohn, R.A., 1996, Geochemistry of ground water in the Gulf Coast aquifer systems, south-central United States: U.S. Geological Survey Water-Resources Investigation Report 96–4107, 158 p.

Price, L.C., 1991, On the origin of the Gulf Coast Neogene oils: Gulf Coast Association of Geological Societies Transactions, v. 41, p. 524–541.

Ramos, A., and Galloway, W.E., 1990, Facies and sand-body geometry of the Queen City (Eocene) tide-dominated delta-margin embayment, northwest Gulf of Mexico basin: Sedimentology, v. 37, p. 1079–1098.

Ricoy, J.U., 1976, Depositional systems in the Sparta Formation (Eocene), Gulf Coast basin of Texas: University of Texas at Austin, M.S. thesis, 98 p.

Ricoy, J.U., and Brown, L.F., Jr., 1977, Depositional systems in the Sparta Formation (Eocene) Gulf Coast basin of Texas: Gulf Coast Association of Geological Societies Transactions, v. 27, p. 103–118.

Rodriguez, R., Sanchez, J.R., Toucet, S., and Hernandez, G., 1995, Deep structure of the southern shelf of Cuba - new implications: American Association of Petroleum Geologists Bulletin, v. 79, no. 13, p. 82.

Rosenfeld, J.H., 2003, Economic potential of the Yucatan block of Mexico, Guatemala, and Belize, in Bartolini, C., Buffler, R.T., and Blickwede, J., eds., The Circum-Gulf of Mexico and the Caribbean - Hydrocarbon habitats, basin formation, and plate tectonics: American Association of Petroleum Geologists Memoir 79, p. 340–348.

Rowan, E.L., Pitman, J.K., and Warwick, P.D., 2007, Thermal maturation history of the Wilcox Group (Paleocene-Eocene), Texas: results of regional-scale multi-1D modeling: Proceedings of the 27th Annual GCSSEPM Bob F. Perkins Research Conference, The Paleogene of the Gulf of Mexico and Caribbean Basins: Processes, Events, and Petroleum Systems, December 2–5, 2007, Houston, Texas, p. 714–743, CD-ROM.

Salvador, A., 1991a, Introduction, in Salvador, A., ed., The Gulf of Mexico Basin: Boulder, Colo., Geological Society of America, The Geology of North America, v. J, p. 1–12.

Salvador, A., 1991b, Origin and development of the Gulf of Mexico basin, in Salvador, A., ed., The Gulf of Mexico Basin: Boulder, Colo., Geological Society of America, The Geology of North America, v. J, p. 389–443.

Salvador, A., and Quezada Muñeton, J.M., 1991, Stratigraphic correlation chart, Gulf of Mexico Basin, in Salvador, A., ed., The Gulf of Mexico Basin: Boulder, Colo., Geological Society of America, The Geology of North America, v. J, plate 5, 1 sheet.

Sams, R.H., 1990, The upper Wilcox-Reklaw marine transgression and its exploration consequences: Bulletin of the South Texas Geological Society, v. 30, no. 9, p. 11–28.

Sassen, R., 1990, Lower Tertiary and Upper Cretaceous source rocks in Louisiana and Mississippi: Implications to Gulf of Mexico crude oil: American Association of Petroleum Geologists Bulletin, v. 74, no. 6, p. 857–878.

Sassen, R., and Moore, C.H., 1988, Framework of hydrocarbon generation and destruction in eastern Smackover trend: American Association of Petroleum Geologists Bulletin, v. 72, p. 649–663.

Sassen, R., Tye, R.S., Chinn, E.W., and Lemoine, R.C., 1988, Origin of crude oil in the Wilcox trend of Louisiana and Mississippi: evidence of long-range migration: Gulf Coast Association of Geological Societies Transactions, v. 38, p. 27–34.

Schenk, C.J., Ahlbrandt, T.S., Charpentier, R.R., Henry, M.E., Klett, T.R., Pollastro, R.M., and Weaver, J.N., 2005, Assessment of undiscovered oil and gas resources of the north Cuba basin, Cuba, 2004: U.S. Geological Survey Fact Sheet 2005–3009, 2 p., CD-ROM, accessed August 15, 2007, at *http://pubs.usgs.gov/fs/2005/3009/*.

Schenk C.J., Higley, D.K., and Magoon, L.B., 2000, Region 6 assessment summary - Central and South America, *in* U.S. Geological Survey world petroleum assessment 2000 - description and results: U.S. Geological Survey Digital Data Series DDS-60, CD-ROM, accessed August 8, 2007, at *http://energy.cr.usgs.gov/WEcont/regions/reg6/R6chap.pdf*.

Schenk, C.J., and Viger, R.J., 1996a, Western Gulf Province (047), *in* Gautier, D.L., Dolton, G.L., Takahashi, K.I., and Varnes, K.L., eds., 1995 national assessment of United States oil and gas resources—Results, methodology, and supporting data: U.S. Geological Survey Digital Data Series DDS-30, version 2, 44 p., accessed August 12, 2007, at *http://certmapper.cr.usgs.gov/data/noga95/prov47/text/prov47.pdf*.

Schenk, C.J., and Viger, R.J., 1996b, East Texas Basin Province (048) and Louisiana-Mississippi Salt Basins Province (049), *in* Gautier, D.L., Dolton, G.L., Takahashi, K.I., and Varnes, K.L., eds., 1995 national assessment of United States oil and gas resources—Results, methodology, and supporting data: U.S. Geological Survey Digital Data Series DDS-30, version 2, 42 p., accessed August 12, 2007, at *http://certmapper.cr.usgs.gov/data/noga95/prov49/text/prov49.pdf*.

Schruben, P.G., Arndt, R.E., Bawiec, W.J., and Ambroziak, R.A., 1994, Geology of the conterminous United States at 1:2,500,000 scale; a digital representation of the 1974 P.B. King and H.M. Beikman map: U.S. Geological Survey Digital Data Series DDS-11, accessed August 24, 2007, at *http://pubs.usgs.gov/dds/dds11/*.

Scott, R.J., 2003, The Maverick basin - new technology - new success, *in* Rosen, N.C. ed., Structure and stratigraphy of south Texas and northeast Mexico, applications to exploration: Society of Economic Paleontologists and Mineralogists, Gulf Coast Section Foundation, and South Texas Geological Society, Houston, Tex., April 11, 2003, p. 84-121, CD-ROM.

Shellman, R.M., 1985, Elm Grove Field, Fayette County, Texas: a case study of shallow, updip Reklaw oil fields in south and central Texas: South Texas Geological Society Bulletin, v. 26, no. 1, p.19–33.

Spooner, W.C., 1926, Interior salt domes of Louisiana: American Association of Petroleum Geologists Bulletin, v. 10, p. 217–292.

Stenzel, H.B., 1939, The Yegua problem: University of Texas Bulletin 3945, p. 847–911.

Stover, S.C., Ge, S., Weimer, P., and McBride, B.C., 2001, The effects of salt evolution, structural development, and fault propagation on Late Mesozoic–Cenozoic oil migration: A two-dimensional fluid-flow study along a megaregional profile in the northern Gulf of Mexico Basin: American Association of Petroleum Geologists Bulletin, v. 85, p. 1945–1966.

Swenson, D.R., 1997, Basal Yegua shelf margin failures along the Texas Gulf coast: Gulf Coast Association of Geological Societies Transactions, v. 47, p. 571–577.

Tellez, M.H., Espiricueto, A., Marino, A., de Leon, J., and Hernández, A., 2002, The gas potential of the Wilcox and Queen City plays in the western Burgos basin, Mexico: Gulf Coast Association of Geological Societies Transactions, v. 52, p. 941.

Tew, B.H., 1992, Sequence stratigraphy, lithofacies relationships, and paleogeography of Oligocene strata in southeastern Mississippi and southwestern Alabama: Alabama Geological Survey Bulletin, no. 146, 73 p.

Thompson, K.F.M., Kennicutt, M.C., II, and Brooks, J.M., 1990, Classification of offshore Gulf of Mexico oils and gas condensates: American Association of Petroleum Geologists Bulletin, v. 74, no. 2, p. 187–198.

Trowbridge, A.C., 1923, A geologic reconnaissance in the Gulf Coastal Plain of Texas, near the Rio Grande, *in* Shorter contributions to general geology, 1922: U.S. Geological Survey Professional Paper, 131-D, p. D85-D107.

Trowbridge, A.C., 1932, Tertiary and Quaternary geology of the lower Rio Grande region of Texas: U.S. Geological Survey Bulletin 837, p. 141–156.

USGS World Energy Assessment Team, 2000, Assessment summary of the Pimienta-Tamabra Total Petroleum System 530501 as part of the 2000 World Petroleum Assessment, *in* U.S. Geological Survey world petroleum assessment 2000 - description and results: U.S. Geological Survey Digital Data Series DDS-60, CD-ROM, accessed August 22, 2007, at *http://energy.cr.usgs.gov/WEcont/regions/reg5/P5/tps/t530501.pdf.*

Vincent, F.S., and Ewing, T.E., 2000, Lower Claiborne regional stratigraphic architecture: southeast Texas to east-central Louisiana: American Association of Petroleum Geologists Bulletin, v. 84, p. 1693.

Wagner, B.E., Sofer, Z., and Claxton, B.L., 1994, Source rock in the Lower Tertiary and Cretaceous, deep-water Gulf of Mexico: Gulf Coast Association of Geological Societies Transactions, v. 44, p. 729–736.

Walters, C.C., and Dusang, D.D., 1988, Source and thermal history of oils from Lockhart Crossing, Livingston Parish, Louisiana: Gulf Coast Association of Geological Societies Transactions, v. 38, p. 37–44.

Warwick, P.D., 2004, Bacterial reduction of CO_2 - the primary origin of low rank coal gas in the northern Gulf of Mexico Coastal Plain, USA: The Society for Organic Petrology 21st Annual Meeting, Abstracts and Program, Sydney, Australia, v. 21, p. 202–204.

Warwick, P.D., 2006, Thermal maturity of the Wilcox Group (Paleocene-Eocene): a key to the Cenozoic petroleum systems of the northern Gulf of Mexico basin, USA: The Society for Organic Petrology 23rd Annual Meeting, Abstracts and Program, Beijing China, v. 23, p. 271–272.

Warwick, P.D., Aubourg, C.A., Hook, R.W., SanFilipo, J.R. (compilers), Morrissey, E.C., Schultz, A.C., Karlsen, A.W., Watt, C.S., Podwysocki, S.M., Mercier, T.J., Wallace, W.C., Tully, J.K., Sun, Zhuang, and Newton, Mathew (digital compilers), 2002, Geology and land use in the western part of the Gulf Coast coal-bearing region: Bureau of Economic Geology, The University of Texas at Austin Miscellaneous Maps 41, 2 sheets 1:500,000 scale, CD-ROM.

Warwick, P.D., Breland, F.C., Jr., and Hackley, P.C., 2008, Biogenic origin of coalbed gas in the northern Gulf of Mexico Coastal Plain, USA: International Journal of Coal Geology, v. 76, p. 119–137.

Warwick, P.D., Coleman, J.L., Hackley, P.C., Hayba, D.O., Karlsen, A.W., Rowan, E.L., and Swanson, S.M., 2007, USGS assessment of undiscovered oil and gas resources in Cenozoic strata of the U.S. Gulf of Mexico Coastal Plain and State waters: Proceedings of the 27th Annual GCSSEPM Bob F. Perkins Research Conference, The Paleogene of the Gulf of Mexico and Caribbean Basins: Processes, Events, and Petroleum Systems, December 2–5, 2007, Houston, Texas, p. 2–44, CD-ROM.

Weatherby, B.B., 1940, The history and development of seismic prospecting: Geophysics, v. 5, no. 3, pt. 1, p. 215–230.

Wendlandt, E.A., and Knebel, G.M., 1926, Lower Claiborne of east Texas, with special reference to Mount Sylvan dome and salt movements: American Association of Petroleum Geologists Bulletin, v. 13, p. 1347–1375.

Wenger, L.M., Goodoff, L.R., Gross, O.P., Harrison, S.C., and Hood, K.C., 1994, Northern Gulf of Mexico: An integrated approach to source, maturation, and migration, *in* Scheidermann, N., Cruz, P., and Sanchez, R. eds., Geologic aspects of petroleum systems: First Joint Meeting of the American Association of Petroleum Geologists and Asociación Mexicana de Geólogos Petroleros, Hedberg Research Conference, 5 p.

Wescott, W.A., and Hood, W.C., 1994, Hydrocarbon generation and migration routes in the East Texas basin: American Association of Petroleum Geologists Bulletin, v. 78, no. 2, p. 287–307.

West, T.S., 1963, Typical stratigraphic traps, Jackson trend of south Texas: Gulf Coast Association of Geological Societies Transactions, v. 13, p. 67–78.

Whitten, C.J., and Berg, R.R., 1987, Depositional environments of downdip Yegua (Eocene) sandstones, Jackson County, Texas: Gulf Coast Association of Geological Societies Transactions, v. 37, p. 513–519.

Winker, C. D., 1982, Cenozoic shelf margins, northwestern Gulf of Mexico: Gulf Coast Association of Geological Societies Transactions, v. 32, p. 427–448.

Witrock, R.B., Friedmann, A.R., Galluzzo, J.J., Nixon, L.D., Post, P.J., and Ross, K.M., 2003, Biostratigraphic chart of the Gulf of Mexico offshore region, Jurassic to Quaternary: U.S. Department of the Interior, Minerals Management Service, New Orleans, 1 sheet.

Zimmerman, R.K., 1999, Potential oil generation capacity of the north Louisiana hydrocarbon system: Gulf Coast Association of Geological Societies Transactions, v. 49, p. 532–540.

Zimmerman, R.K., 2000, Stratigraphic zone-depth predictions for Louisiana's probable hydrocarbon exploration floor: Gulf Coast Association of Geological Societies Transactions, v. 50 (L), p. 505–507.

Zimmerman, R.K., and Sassen, R., 1993, Hydrocarbon transfer pathways from Smackover source rocks to younger reservoir traps in the Monroe gas field, northeast Louisiana: Gulf Coast Association of Geological Societies Transactions, v. 43, p. 473–480.

Appendixes A-G

Appendix A. Input data for the Lower Claiborne Stable Shelf Gas and Oil Assessment Unit (50470120). Seventh Approximation Data Form for Conventional Assessment Units (Version 6, 9 April, 2003). Abbreviations: AU = assessment unit; cfg/bo = cubic feet of gas per barrel of oil; mmboe = million barrels of oil equivalent; accums. = accumulations; mmbo = million barrels of oil; bcfg = billion cubic feet of gas; min. = minimum; max. = maximum; bngl/mmcfg = barrels of natural gas liquids per million cubic feet of gas; bliq/mmcfg = barrels of liquid per million cubic feet of gas; bo/mmcfg = barrels of oil per million cubic feet of natural gas; % = percent; m = meters.

SEVENTH APPROXIMATION
DATA FORM FOR CONVENTIONAL ASSESSMENT UNITS (Version 6, 9 April 2003)

IDENTIFICATION INFORMATION

Assessment Geologist:	P.C. Hackley	Date:	22-Jan-07
Region:	North America	Number:	5
Province:	Western Gulf	Number:	5047
Total Petroleum System:	Upper Jurassic-Cretaceous-Tertiary Composite	Number:	504701
Assessment Unit:	Lower Claiborne Stable Shelf Gas and Oil	Number:	50470120
Based on Data as of:	NRG 2006 (data current through 2004), IHS 2005 (data current through 2005)		
Notes from Assessor:	NRG reservoir growth factor		

CHARACTERISTICS OF ASSESSMENT UNIT

Oil (<20,000 cfg/bo overall) **or** Gas (≥20,000 cfg/bo overall):   Gas

What is the minimum accumulation size?   0.5   mmboe grown
(the smallest accumulation that has potential to be added to reserves)

No. of discovered accumulations exceeding minimum size: Oil: 16   Gas: 39
Established (>13 accums.)   X   Frontier (1-13 accums.)   Hypothetical (no accums.)

Median size (grown) of discovered oil accumulations (mmbo):
                1st 3rd   1.46   2nd 3rd   2.84   3rd 3rd   1.56
Median size (grown) of discovered gas accumulations (bcfg):
                1st 3rd   13.39   2nd 3rd   7.72   3rd 3rd   5.21

Assessment-Unit Probabilities:

Attribute	Probability of occurrence (0-1.0)
1. **CHARGE:** Adequate petroleum charge for an undiscovered accum. ≥ minimum size:	1.0
2. **ROCKS:** Adequate reservoirs, traps, and seals for an undiscovered accum. ≥ minimum size:	1.0
3. **TIMING OF GEOLOGIC EVENTS:** Favorable timing for an undiscovered accum. ≥ minimum siz	1.0

Assessment-Unit GEOLOGIC Probability (Product of 1, 2, and 3):   1.0

UNDISCOVERED ACCUMULATIONS

No. of Undiscovered Accumulations: How many undiscovered accums. exist that are ≥ min. size?:
                (uncertainty of fixed but unknown values)

Oil Accumulations:	minimum (>0) 1	mode 5	maximum 15
Gas Accumulations:	minimum (>0) 1	mode 10	maximum 30

Sizes of Undiscovered Accumulations: What are the sizes (**grown**) of the above accums.?:
                (variations in the sizes of undiscovered accumulations)

Oil in Oil Accumulations (mmbo):	minimum 0.5	median 1	maximum 3
Gas in Gas Accumulations (bcfg):	minimum 3	median 4	maximum 40

Assessment Unit (name, no.)
Lower Claiborne Stable Shelf Gas and Oil, 50470120

AVERAGE RATIOS FOR UNDISCOVERED ACCUMS., TO ASSESS COPRODUCTS
(uncertainty of fixed but unknown values)

Oil Accumulations:	minimum	mode	maximum
Gas/oil ratio (cfg/bo)	1400	2800	4200
NGL/gas ratio (bngl/mmcfg)	11	22	33

Gas Accumulations:	minimum	mode	maximum
Liquids/gas ratio (bliq/mmcfg)	12.7	25.4	38.1
Oil/gas ratio (bo/mmcfg)			

SELECTED ANCILLARY DATA FOR UNDISCOVERED ACCUMULATIONS
(variations in the properties of undiscovered accumulations)

Oil Accumulations:	minimum		mode		maximum
API gravity (degrees)	19		38		46
Sulfur content of oil (%)	0		0.1		0.2
Depth (m) of water (if applicable)					

	minimum	F75	mode	F25	maximum
Drilling Depth (m)	24	1030	1610	1690	2520

Gas Accumulations:	minimum		mode		maximum
Inert gas content (%)	0		0.5		1.1
CO_2 content (%)	0.2		1.6		2.8
Hydrogen-sulfide content (%)	0		0		0
Depth (m) of water (if applicable)					

	minimum	F75	mode	F25	maximum
Drilling Depth (m)	280	1660	1900	2250	3660

Appendix B. Input data for the Lower Claiborne Expanded Fault Zone Gas assessment unit (50470121). Seventh Approximation Data Form for Conventional Assessment Units (Version 6, 9 April, 2003). Abbreviations: AU = assessment unit; cfg/bo = cubic feet of gas per barrel of oil; mmboe = million barrels of oil equivalent; accums. = accumulations; mmbo = million barrels of oil; bcfg = billion cubic feet of gas; min. = minimum; max. = maximum; bngl/mmcfg = barrels of natural gas liquids per million cubic feet of gas; bliq/mmcfg = barrels of liquid per million cubic feet of gas; bo/mmcfg = barrels of oil per million cubic feet of natural gas; % = percent; m = meters.

SEVENTH APPROXIMATION
DATA FORM FOR CONVENTIONAL ASSESSMENT UNITS (Version 6, 9 April 2003)

IDENTIFICATION INFORMATION

Assessment Geologist:	P.C. Hackley	Date:	23-Jan-07
Region:	North America	Number:	5
Province:	Western Gulf	Number:	5047
Total Petroleum System:	Upper Jurassic-Cretaceous-Tertiary Composite	Number:	504701
Assessment Unit:	Lower Claiborne Expanded Fault Zone Gas	Number:	50470121
Based on Data as of:	NRG 2006 (data current through 2004), IHS 2005 (data current through 2005)		
Notes from Assessor:	NRG reservoir growth factor		

CHARACTERISTICS OF ASSESSMENT UNIT

Oil (<20,000 cfg/bo overall) **or** Gas (≥20,000 cfg/bo overall):   Gas

What is the minimum accumulation size?   0.5   mmboe grown
(the smallest accumulation that has potential to be added to reserves)

No. of discovered accumulations exceeding minimum size: Oil: 0   Gas: 10
Established (>13 accums.) _____ Frontier (1-13 accums.)   X   Hypothetical (no accums.) _____

Median size (grown) of discovered oil accumulations (mmbo):
          1st 3rd _____   2nd 3rd _____   3rd 3rd _____
Median size (grown) of discovered gas accumulations (bcfg):
          1st 3rd   9.7   2nd 3rd   35.1   3rd 3rd _____

Assessment-Unit Probabilities:

Attribute	Probability of occurrence (0-1.0)
1. **CHARGE:** Adequate petroleum charge for an undiscovered accum. ≥ minimum size:	1.0
2. **ROCKS:** Adequate reservoirs, traps, and seals for an undiscovered accum. ≥ minimum size:	1.0
3. **TIMING OF GEOLOGIC EVENTS:** Favorable timing for an undiscovered accum. ≥ minimum size	1.0

Assessment-Unit GEOLOGIC Probability (Product of 1, 2, and 3):   1.0

UNDISCOVERED ACCUMULATIONS

No. of Undiscovered Accumulations: How many undiscovered accums. exist that are ≥ min. size?:
(uncertainty of fixed but unknown values)

Oil Accumulations:	minimum (>0)	1	mode	2	maximum	5
Gas Accumulations:	minimum (>0)	5	mode	25	maximum	50

Sizes of Undiscovered Accumulations: What are the sizes (**grown**) of the above accums.?:
(variations in the sizes of undiscovered accumulations)

Oil in Oil Accumulations (mmbo):	minimum	0.5	median	1	maximum	15
Gas in Gas Accumulations (bcfg):	minimum	3	median	20	maximum	700

Appendix B. Input data for the Lower Claiborne Expanded Fault Zone Gas assessment unit (50470121) continued.

Assessment Unit (name, no.)
Lower Claiborne Expanded Fault Zone Gas, 50470121

AVERAGE RATIOS FOR UNDISCOVERED ACCUMS., TO ASSESS COPRODUCTS
(uncertainty of fixed but unknown values)

Oil Accumulations:	minimum	mode	maximum
Gas/oil ratio (cfg/bo)	2560	5125	7690
NGL/gas ratio (bngl/mmcfg)	35	70	105

Gas Accumulations:	minimum	mode	maximum
Liquids/gas ratio (bliq/mmcfg)	20	40	60
Oil/gas ratio (bo/mmcfg)			

SELECTED ANCILLARY DATA FOR UNDISCOVERED ACCUMULATIONS
(variations in the properties of undiscovered accumulations)

Oil Accumulations:	minimum	mode	maximum
API gravity (degrees)	35	49	55
Sulfur content of oil (%)	0	0.1	0.4
Depth (m) of water (if applicable)			

	minimum	F75	mode	F25	maximum
Drilling Depth (m)	1524		2438		4267

Gas Accumulations:	minimum	mode	maximum
Inert gas content (%)	0	0.5	2.4
CO_2 content (%)	0.5	1.2	3.4
Hydrogen-sulfide content (%)	0	0.1	0.2
Depth (m) of water (if applicable)			

	minimum	F75	mode	F25	maximum
Drilling Depth (m)	1524		2957		4267

Appendix C. Input data for the Lower Claiborne Slope and Basin Floor Gas assessment unit (50470122). Seventh Approximation Data Form for Conventional Assessment Units (Version 6, 9 April, 2003). Abbreviations: AU = assessment unit; cfg/bo = cubic feet of gas per barrel of oil; mmboe = million barrels of oil equivalent; accums. = accumulations; mmbo = million barrels of oil; bcfg = billion cubic feet of gas; min. = minimum; max. = maximum; bngl/mmcfg = barrels of natural gas liquids per million cubic feet of gas; bliq/mmcfg = barrels of liquid per million cubic feet of gas; bo/mmcfg = barrels of oil per million cubic feet of natural gas; % = percent; m = meters.

SEVENTH APPROXIMATION
DATA FORM FOR CONVENTIONAL ASSESSMENT UNITS (Version 6, 9 April 2003)

IDENTIFICATION INFORMATION

Assessment Geologist:	P.C. Hackley	Date:	23-Jan-07
Region:	North America	Number:	5
Province:	Western Gulf	Number:	5047
Total Petroleum System:	Upper Jurassic-Cretaceous-Tertiary Composite	Number:	504701
Assessment Unit:	Lower Claiborne Slope and Basin Floor Gas	Number:	50470122
Based on Data as of:	NRG 2006 (data current through 2004), IHS 2005 (data current through 2005)		
Notes from Assessor:	NRG reservoir growth factor. Lower Miocene Slope and Basin Gas, Assessment		
	Unit 50470141 and its Federal offshore extension and scaled-down Wilcox		
	Slope and Basin Floor Gas, Assessment Unit 50470118 were used as analogs.		

CHARACTERISTICS OF ASSESSMENT UNIT

Oil (<20,000 cfg/bo overall) **or** Gas (≥20,000 cfg/bo overall): ___Gas___

What is the minimum accumulation size? ___0.5___ mmboe grown
(the smallest accumulation that has potential to be added to reserves)

No. of discovered accumulations exceeding minimum size: Oil: __0__ Gas: __0__
Established (>13 accums.) _____ Frontier (1-13 accums.) _____ Hypothetical (no accums __X__

Median size (grown) of discovered oil accumulations (mmbo):
      1st 3rd _____ 2nd 3rd _____ 3rd 3rd _____
Median size (grown) of discovered gas accumulations (bcfg):
      1st 3rd _____ 2nd 3rd _____ 3rd 3rd _____

Assessment-Unit Probabilities:

Attribute	Probability of occurrence (0-1.0)
1. **CHARGE:** Adequate petroleum charge for an undiscovered accum. ≥ minimum size:	1.0
2. **ROCKS:** Adequate reservoirs, traps, and seals for an undiscovered accum. ≥ minimum size:	1.0
3. **TIMING OF GEOLOGIC EVENTS:** Favorable timing for an undiscovered accum. ≥ minimum size	1.0

Assessment-Unit GEOLOGIC Probability (Product of 1, 2, and 3): ___1.0___

UNDISCOVERED ACCUMULATIONS
No. of Undiscovered Accumulations: How many undiscovered accums. exist that are ≥ min. size?:
      (uncertainty of fixed but unknown values)

Oil Accumulations:	minimum (>0)	0	mode	0	maximum	0
Gas Accumulations:	minimum (>0)	1	mode	20	maximum	200

Sizes of Undiscovered Accumulations: What are the sizes (**grown**) of the above accums?:
      (variations in the sizes of undiscovered accumulations)

Oil in Oil Accumulations (mmbo):	minimum		median		maximum	
Gas in Gas Accumulations (bcfg):	minimum	3	median	20	maximum	1500

Appendix C. Input data for the Lower Claiborne Slope and Basin Floor Gas assessment unit (50470122) continued.

Assessment Unit (name, no.)
Lower Claiborne Slope and Basin Floor Gas, 50470122

AVERAGE RATIOS FOR UNDISCOVERED ACCUMS., TO ASSESS COPRODUCTS
(uncertainty of fixed but unknown values)

Oil Accumulations:	minimum	mode	maximum
Gas/oil ratio (cfg/bo)	_____	_____	_____
NGL/gas ratio (bngl/mmcfg)	_____	_____	_____
Gas Accumulations:	minimum	mode	maximum
Liquids/gas ratio (bliq/mmcfg)	20	40	60
Oil/gas ratio (bo/mmcfg)	_____	_____	_____

SELECTED ANCILLARY DATA FOR UNDISCOVERED ACCUMULATIONS
(variations in the properties of undiscovered accumulations)

Oil Accumulations:	minimum		mode		maximum
API gravity (degrees)	_____		_____		_____
Sulfur content of oil (%)	_____		_____		_____
Depth (m) of water (if applicable)	_____		_____		_____
	minimum	F75	mode	F25	maximum
Drilling Depth (m)					

Gas Accumulations:	minimum		mode		maximum
Inert gas content (%)	0		0.5		2.4
CO_2 content (%)	0.5		1.2		3.4
Hydrogen-sulfide content (%)	0		0.1		0.2
Depth (m) of water (if applicable)	0		10		50
	minimum	F75	mode	F25	maximum
Drilling Depth (m)	3658	4267	4877	6096	9144

Appendix D. Input data for the Lower Claiborne Cane River assessment unit (50470123). Seventh Approximation Data Form for Conventional Assessment Units (Version 6, 9 April, 2003). Abbreviations: AU = assessment unit; cfg/bo = cubic feet of gas per barrel of oil; mmboe = million barrels of oil equivalent; accums. = accumulations; mmbo = million barrels of oil; bcfg = billion cubic feet of gas; min. = minimum; max. = maximum; bngl/mmcfg = barrels of natural gas liquids per million cubic feet of gas; bliq/mmcfg = barrels of liquid per million cubic feet of gas; bo/mmcfg = barrels of oil per million cubic feet of natural gas; % = percent; m = meters.

SEVENTH APPROXIMATION
DATA FORM FOR CONVENTIONAL ASSESSMENT UNITS (Version 6, 9 April 2003)

IDENTIFICATION INFORMATION

Assessment Geologist:	P.C. Hackley	Date:	23-Jan-07
Region:	North America	Number:	5
Province:	Western Gulf	Number:	5047
Total Petroleum System:	Upper Jurassic-Cretaceous-Tertiary Composite	Number:	504701
Assessment Unit:	Lower Claiborne Cane River	Number:	50470123
Based on Data as of:	NRG 2006 (data current through 2004), IHS 2005 (data current through 2005)		
Notes from Assessor:	Not quantitatively assessed.		

CHARACTERISTICS OF ASSESSMENT UNIT

Oil (<20,000 cfg/bo overall) **or** Gas (≥20,000 cfg/bo overall): _____

What is the minimum accumulation size? _____ mmboe grown
(the smallest accumulation that has potential to be added to reserves)

No. of discovered accumulations exceeding minimum size: Oil: _____   Gas: _____
Established (>13 accums.) _____ Frontier (1-13 accums.) _____ Hypothetical (no accums.) _____

Median size (grown) of discovered oil accumulations (mmbo):
                          1st 3rd _____ 2nd 3rd _____ 3rd 3rd _____
Median size (grown) of discovered gas accumulations (bcfg):
                          1st 3rd _____ 2nd 3rd _____ 3rd 3rd _____

Assessment-Unit Probabilities:
  Attribute   Probability of occurrence (0-1.0)
1. **CHARGE:** Adequate petroleum charge for an undiscovered accum. ≥ minimum size: _____
2. **ROCKS:** Adequate reservoirs, traps, and seals for an undiscovered accum. ≥ minimum size: _____
3. **TIMING OF GEOLOGIC EVENTS:** Favorable timing for an undiscovered accum. ≥ minimum size: _____

Assessment-Unit GEOLOGIC Probability (Product of 1, 2, and 3): _____

UNDISCOVERED ACCUMULATIONS
No. of Undiscovered Accumulations: How many undiscovered accums. exist that are ≥ min. size?:
                          (uncertainty of fixed but unknown values)

Oil Accumulations:	minimum (>0) _____	mode _____	maximum _____
Gas Accumulations:	minimum (>0) _____	mode _____	maximum _____

Sizes of Undiscovered Accumulations: What are the sizes (**grown**) of the above accums.?:
                          (variations in the sizes of undiscovered accumulations)

Oil in Oil Accumulations (mmbo):	minimum _____	median _____	maximum _____
Gas in Gas Accumulations (bcfg):	minimum _____	median _____	maximum _____

Assessment Unit (name, no.)
Lower Claiborne Cane River, 50470123

AVERAGE RATIOS FOR UNDISCOVERED ACCUMS., TO ASSESS COPRODUCTS
(uncertainty of fixed but unknown values)

Oil Accumulations:	minimum	mode	maximum
Gas/oil ratio (cfg/bo)	_____	_____	_____
NGL/gas ratio (bngl/mmcfg)	_____	_____	_____

Gas Accumulations:	minimum	mode	maximum
Liquids/gas ratio (bliq/mmcfg)	_____	_____	_____
Oil/gas ratio (bo/mmcfg)	_____	_____	_____

SELECTED ANCILLARY DATA FOR UNDISCOVERED ACCUMULATIONS
(variations in the properties of undiscovered accumulations)

Oil Accumulations:	minimum	mode	maximum
API gravity (degrees)	_____	_____	_____
Sulfur content of oil (%)	_____	_____	_____
Depth (m) of water (if applicable)	_____	_____	_____

	minimum	F75	mode	F25	maximum
Drilling Depth (m)					

Gas Accumulations:	minimum	mode	maximum
Inert gas content (%)	_____	_____	_____
CO_2 content (%)	_____	_____	_____
Hydrogen-sulfide content (%)	_____	_____	_____
Depth (m) of water (if applicable)	_____	_____	_____

	minimum	F75	mode	F25	maximum
Drilling Depth (m)					

81

Appendix E. Input data for the Upper Claiborne Stable Shelf Gas and Oil assessment unit (50470124). Seventh Approximation Data Form for Conventional Assessment Units (Version 6, 9 April, 2003). Abbreviations: AU = assessment unit; cfg/bo = cubic feet of gas per barrel of oil; mmboe = million barrels of oil equivalent; accums. = accumulations; mmbo = million barrels of oil; bcfg = billion cubic feet of gas; min. = minimum; max. = maximum; bngl/mmcfg = barrels of natural gas liquids per million cubic feet of gas; bliq/mmcfg = barrels of liquid per million cubic feet of gas; bo/mmcfg = barrels of oil per million cubic feet of natural gas; % = percent; m = meters.

SEVENTH APPROXIMATION
DATA FORM FOR CONVENTIONAL ASSESSMENT UNITS (Version 6, 9 April 2003)

IDENTIFICATION INFORMATION

Assessment Geologist:	P.C. Hackley	Date:	23-Jan-07
Region:	North America	Number:	5
Province:	Western Gulf	Number:	5047
Total Petroleum System:	Upper Jurassic-Cretaceous-Tertiary Composite	Number:	504701
Assessment Unit:	Upper Claiborne Stable Shelf Gas and Oil	Number:	50470124
Based on Data as of:	NRG 2006 (data current through 2004), IHS 2005 (data current through 2005)		
Notes from Assessor:	NRG reservoir growth factor		

CHARACTERISTICS OF ASSESSMENT UNIT

Oil (<20,000 cfg/bo overall) **or** Gas (>20,000 cfg/bo overall):   Oil

What is the minimum accumulation size?   0.5   mmboe grown
(the smallest accumulation that has potential to be added to reserves)

No. of discovered accumulations exceeding minimum size: Oil: 175   Gas: 153
Established (>13 accums.)   X   Frontier (1-13 accums.) _____   Hypothetical (no accums.) _____

Median size (grown) of discovered oil accumulations (mmbo):
    1st 3rd 2.12   2nd 3rd 1.71   3rd 3rd 1.15
Median size (grown) of discovered gas accumulations (bcfg):
    1st 3rd 14.49   2nd 3rd 7.14   3rd 3rd 8.7

Assessment-Unit Probabilities:

Attribute	Probability of occurrence (0-1.0)
1. **CHARGE:** Adequate petroleum charge for an undiscovered accum. > minimum size:	1.0
2. **ROCKS:** Adequate reservoirs, traps, and seals for an undiscovered accum. > minimum size:	1.0
3. **TIMING OF GEOLOGIC EVENTS:** Favorable timing for an undiscovered accum. > minimum size	1.0
Assessment-Unit GEOLOGIC Probability (Product of 1, 2, and 3):	1.0

UNDISCOVERED ACCUMULATIONS
No. of Undiscovered Accumulations: How many undiscovered accums. exist that are > min. size?:
(uncertainty of fixed but unknown values)

Oil Accumulations:	minimum (>0)	1	mode	10	maximum	30
Gas Accumulations:	minimum (>0)	4	mode	15	maximum	75

Sizes of Undiscovered Accumulations: What are the sizes (**grown**) of the above accums.?:
(variations in the sizes of undiscovered accumulations)

Oil in Oil Accumulations (mmbo):	minimum	0.5	median	0.8	maximum	5
Gas in Gas Accumulations (bcfg):	minimum	3	median	6	maximum	400

Assessment Unit (name, no.)
Upper Claiborne Stable Shelf Gas and Oil, 50470124

AVERAGE RATIOS FOR UNDISCOVERED ACCUMS., TO ASSESS COPRODUCTS
(uncertainty of fixed but unknown values)

Oil Accumulations:	minimum	mode	maximum
Gas/oil ratio (cfg/bo)	1550	3100	4650
NGL/gas ratio (bngl/mmcfg)	10	20	30

Gas Accumulations:	minimum	mode	maximum
Liquids/gas ratio (bliq/mmcfg)	14	28	42
Oil/gas ratio (bo/mmcfg)			

SELECTED ANCILLARY DATA FOR UNDISCOVERED ACCUMULATIONS
(variations in the properties of undiscovered accumulations)

Oil Accumulations:	minimum	mode	maximum
API gravity (degrees)	17	40	55
Sulfur content of oil (%)	0	0.1	0.4
Depth (m) of water (if applicable)	0	10	20

	minimum	F75	mode	F25	maximum
Drilling Depth (m)	304	1170	1615	1981	3475

Gas Accumulations:	minimum	mode	maximum
Inert gas content (%)	0	0.5	8.4
CO_2 content (%)	0.1	0.6	2.4
Hydrogen-sulfide content (%)	0	0.1	0.2
Depth (m) of water (if applicable)	0	10	20

	minimum	F75	mode	F25	maximum
Drilling Depth (m)	304	1591	2100	2450	3475

Appendix F. Input data for the Upper Claiborne Expanded Fault Zone Gas assessment unit (50470125). Seventh Approximation Data Form for Conventional Assessment Units (Version 6, 9 April, 2003). Abbreviations: AU = assessment unit; cfg/bo = cubic feet of gas per barrel of oil; mmboe = million barrels of oil equivalent; accums. = accumulations; mmbo = million barrels of oil; bcfg = billion cubic feet of gas; min. = minimum; max. = maximum; bngl/mmcfg = barrels of natural gas liquids per million cubic feet of gas; bliq/mmcfg = barrels of liquid per million cubic feet of gas; bo/mmcfg = barrels of oil per million cubic feet of natural gas; % = percent; m = meters.

SEVENTH APPROXIMATION
DATA FORM FOR CONVENTIONAL ASSESSMENT UNITS (Version 6, 9 April 2003)

IDENTIFICATION INFORMATION

Assessment Geologist:	P.C. Hackley	Date:	23-Jan-07
Region:	North America	Number:	5
Province:	Western Gulf	Number:	5047
Total Petroleum System:	Upper Jurassic-Cretaceous-Tertiary Composite	Number:	504701
Assessment Unit:	Upper Claiborne Expanded Fault Zone Gas	Number:	50470125
Based on Data as of:	NRG 2006 (data current through 2004), IHS 2005 (data current through 2005)		
Notes from Assessor:	NRG reservoir growth factor		

CHARACTERISTICS OF ASSESSMENT UNIT

Oil (<20,000 cfg/bo overall) **or** Gas (≥20,000 cfg/bo overall): _____Gas_____

What is the minimum accumulation size? _____0.5_____ mmboe grown
(the smallest accumulation that has potential to be added to reserves)

No. of discovered accumulations exceeding minimum size: Oil: _____11_____ Gas: _____97_____
Established (>13 accums.) _____X_____ Frontier (1-13 accums.) _____ Hypothetical (no accums.) _____

Median size (grown) of discovered oil accumulations (mmbo):
　　　　　　1st 3rd _____2.43_____ 2nd 3rd _____1.89_____ 3rd 3rd _____
Median size (grown) of discovered gas accumulations (bcfg):
　　　　　　1st 3rd _____23.48_____ 2nd 3rd _____23.5_____ 3rd 3rd _____25.56_____

Assessment-Unit Probabilities:

Attribute	Probability of occurrence (0-1.0)
1. **CHARGE:** Adequate petroleum charge for an undiscovered accum. ≥ minimum size:	1.0
2. **ROCKS:** Adequate reservoirs, traps, and seals for an undiscovered accum. ≥ minimum size:	1.0
3. **TIMING OF GEOLOGIC EVENTS:** Favorable timing for an undiscovered accum. ≥ minimum size	1.0

Assessment-Unit GEOLOGIC Probability (Product of 1, 2, and 3): _____1.0_____

UNDISCOVERED ACCUMULATIONS

No. of Undiscovered Accumulations: How many undiscovered accums. exist that are ≥ min. size?:
　　　　　　　　　(uncertainty of fixed but unknown values)

Oil Accumulations:	minimum (>0)	1	mode	10	maximum	40
Gas Accumulations:	minimum (>0)	10	mode	90	maximum	360

Sizes of Undiscovered Accumulations: What are the sizes (**grown**) of the above accums.?:
　　　　　　　　　(variations in the sizes of undiscovered accumulations)

Oil in Oil Accumulations (mmbo):	minimum	0.5	median	1.5	maximum	5
Gas in Gas Accumulations (bcfg):	minimum	3	median	20	maximum	400

Appendix F. Input data for the Upper Claiborne Expanded Fault Zone Gas assessment unit (50470125) continued.

Assessment Unit (name, no.)
Upper Claiborne Expanded Fault Zone Gas, 50470125

AVERAGE RATIOS FOR UNDISCOVERED ACCUMS., TO ASSESS COPRODUCTS
(uncertainty of fixed but unknown values)

Oil Accumulations:	minimum	mode	maximum
Gas/oil ratio (cfg/bo)	2560	5125	7690
NGL/gas ratio (bngl/mmcfg)	35	70	105

Gas Accumulations:	minimum	mode	maximum
Liquids/gas ratio (bliq/mmcfg)	36	72	108
Oil/gas ratio (bo/mmcfg)			

SELECTED ANCILLARY DATA FOR UNDISCOVERED ACCUMULATIONS
(variations in the properties of undiscovered accumulations)

Oil Accumulations:	minimum	mode	maximum
API gravity (degrees)	35	49	55
Sulfur content of oil (%)	0	0.1	0.4
Depth (m) of water (if applicable)	0	10	20

	minimum	F75	mode	F25	maximum
Drilling Depth (m)	1524		2987		4267

Gas Accumulations:	minimum	mode	maximum
Inert gas content (%)	0	0.5	2.4
CO_2 content (%)	0.5	1.2	3.4
Hydrogen-sulfide content (%)	0	0.1	0.2
Depth (m) of water (if applicable)	0	10	20

	minimum	F75	mode	F25	maximum
Drilling Depth (m)	1524		3353		4877

Appendix G. Input data for the Upper Claiborne Slope and Basin Floor Gas assessment unit (50470126). Seventh Approximation Data Form for Conventional Assessment Units (Version 6, 9 April, 2003). Abbreviations: AU = assessment unit; cfg/bo = cubic feet of gas per barrel of oil; mmboe = million barrels of oil equivalent; accums. = accumulations; mmbo = million barrels of oil; bcfg = billion cubic feet of gas; min. = minimum; max. = maximum; bngl/mmcfg = barrels of natural gas liquids per million cubic feet of gas; bliq/mmcfg = barrels of liquid per million cubic feet of gas; bo/mmcfg = barrels of oil per million cubic feet of natural gas; % = percent; m = meters.

SEVENTH APPROXIMATION
DATA FORM FOR CONVENTIONAL ASSESSMENT UNITS (Version 6, 9 April 2003)

IDENTIFICATION INFORMATION

Assessment Geologist:	P.C. Hackley	Date:	23-Jan-07
Region:	North America	Number:	5
Province:	Western Gulf	Number:	5047
Total Petroleum System:	Upper Jurassic-Cretaceous-Tertiary Composite	Number:	504701
Assessment Unit:	Upper Claiborne Slope and Basin Floor Gas	Number:	50470126
Based on Data as of:	NRG 2006 (data current through 2004), IHS 2005 (data current through 2005)		
Notes from Assessor:	NRG reservoir growth factor. Lower Miocene Slope and Basin Gas, Assessment		
	Unit 50470141 and its Federal offshore extension and scaled-down Wilcox		
	Slope and Basin Floor Gas, Assessment Unit 50470118 were used as analogs.		

CHARACTERISTICS OF ASSESSMENT UNIT

Oil (<20,000 cfg/bo overall) **or** Gas (≥20,000 cfg/bo overall):   Gas

What is the minimum accumulation size?   0.5   mmboe grown
(the smallest accumulation that has potential to be added to reserves)

No. of discovered accumulations exceeding minimum size: Oil: 0   Gas: 0
Established (>13 accums.) _____   Frontier (1-13 accums.) _____   Hypothetical (no accums   X

Median size (grown) of discovered oil accumulations (mmbo):
        1st 3rd _____   2nd 3rd _____   3rd 3rd _____
Median size (grown) of discovered gas accumulations (bcfg):
        1st 3rd _____   2nd 3rd _____   3rd 3rd _____

Assessment-Unit Probabilities:

Attribute	Probability of occurrence (0-1.0)
1. **CHARGE:** Adequate petroleum charge for an undiscovered accum. ≥ minimum size:	1.0
2. **ROCKS:** Adequate reservoirs, traps, and seals for an undiscovered accum. ≥ minimum size:	1.0
3. **TIMING OF GEOLOGIC EVENTS:** Favorable timing for an undiscovered accum. ≥ minimum size	1.0

Assessment-Unit GEOLOGIC Probability (Product of 1, 2, and 3):   1.0

UNDISCOVERED ACCUMULATIONS
No. of Undiscovered Accumulations: How many undiscovered accums. exist that are ≥ min. size?:
        (uncertainty of fixed but unknown values)

Oil Accumulations:	minimum (>0)	0	mode	0	maximum	0
Gas Accumulations:	minimum (>0)	5	mode	50	maximum	500

Sizes of Undiscovered Accumulations: What are the sizes (**grown**) of the above accums.?:
        (variations in the sizes of undiscovered accumulations)

Oil in Oil Accumulations (mmbo):	minimum		median		maximum	
Gas in Gas Accumulations (bcfg):	minimum	3	median	20	maximum	1500

Assessment Unit (name, no.)
Upper Claiborne Slope and Basin Floor Gas, 50470126

AVERAGE RATIOS FOR UNDISCOVERED ACCUMS., TO ASSESS COPRODUCTS
(uncertainty of fixed but unknown values)

Oil Accumulations:	minimum	mode	maximum
Gas/oil ratio (cfg/bo)	_____	_____	_____
NGL/gas ratio (bngl/mmcfg)	_____	_____	_____
Gas Accumulations:	minimum	mode	maximum
Liquids/gas ratio (bliq/mmcfg)	36	72	108
Oil/gas ratio (bo/mmcfg)	_____	_____	_____

SELECTED ANCILLARY DATA FOR UNDISCOVERED ACCUMULATIONS
(variations in the properties of undiscovered accumulations)

Oil Accumulations:	minimum		mode		maximum
API gravity (degrees)	_____		_____		_____
Sulfur content of oil (%)	_____		_____		_____
Depth (m) of water (if applicable)	_____		_____		_____
	minimum	F75	mode	F25	maximum
Drilling Depth (m)					

Gas Accumulations:	minimum		mode		maximum
Inert gas content (%)	0		0.5		2.4
CO_2 content (%)	0.5		1.2		3.4
Hydrogen-sulfide content (%)	0		0.1		0.2
Depth (m) of water (if applicable)	0		10		50
	minimum	F75	mode	F25	maximum
Drilling Depth (m)	3658		4938		9144